O CHRISTMAS TREE!

JACK MAGUIRE

AVON BOOKS ◆ NEW YORK

O CHRISTMAS TREE! is an original publication of Avon Books. This work has never before appeared in book form.

AVON BOOKS
A division of
The Hearst Corporation
1350 Avenue of the Americas
New York, New York 10019

Allen County Public Library
900 Webster Street
PO Box 2270
Fort Wayne, IN 46801-2270

Copyright © 1992 by Jack Maguire
Published by arrangement with the author
Library of Congress Catalog Card Number: 92-24144
ISBN: 0-380-77070-9

Library of Congress Cataloging in Publication Data:

Maguire, Jack.
    O Christmas tree! / Jack Maguire.
       p.   cm.
    1. Christmas trees—History. 2. Christmas stories. I. Title.
GT4989.M34   1992   92-24144
394.2'68282—dc20   CIP

First Avon Books Trade Printing: November 1992

AVON TRADEMARK REG. U.S. PAT. OFF. AND IN OTHER COUNTRIES, MARCA REGISTRADA, HECHO EN U.S.A.

Printed in the U.S.A.

ARC 10 9 8 7 6 5 4 3 2 1

This book is dedicated to Debbi Sheeley,
a lover of Christmas trees
and a gift of a friend.

I thank Jody Rein, my editor, and Faith Hamlin, my agent,
for all their help in making this book happen.

Contents

Contents

Preface

Why are we so mysteriously soothed by the sight of an evergreen tree inside our homes at Christmastime? Perhaps it's because the color, texture, bulk, and fragrance of the tree combine to stir deep memories of our ancestral communion with nature. And placing it in the center of our day-to-day life recalls the way we once depended on its close, vital presence to shelter our bodies and sustain our spirits during the long winter months.

The decorated evergreen tree is not only one of the most beloved images associated with the Christmas season, it is also one of the richest in cultural significance. Many different social and religious beliefs and practices, some of them dating several centuries before the birth of Christ, have contributed to the origin of the Christmas tree. In turn, the Christmas tree has inspired a wealth of customs and stories in its own right.

O Christmas Tree! explores the fascinating history and fantasy surrounding this beloved symbol. Give yourself a gift, and get to know more about the wondrous and powerful spell that the Christmas tree casts over all who stand before it!

O Tannenbaum! ❄ O Christmas Tree!

(an old German carol, perhaps adapted from a Catholic hymn)

❄   ❄   ❄

We stand before the Christmas tree,
A symbol for the faithful.
We stand before the Christmas tree,
A symbol for the faithful.
Its foliage green will always grow
Through summer sun and winter snow.
We stand before the Christmas tree,
A symbol for the faithful.

O Tannenbaum, O Tannenbaum,
Wie treu sind deine Blatter!
O Tannenbaum, O Tannenbaum,
Wie treu sind deine Blatter!
Du grunst nicht nur zur Sommerszeit,
Nein, auch im Winter, wenn es schneit.
O Tannenbaum, O Tannenbaum,
Wie treu sind deine Blatter!

How the Christmas Tree Came to Be

$\mathfrak{S}$tanding unadorned in a meadow, field, or forest, a mature evergreen tree not only delights the eye, with its trim green needles and pleasing symmetry, but also speaks to the soul. It bears itself like a steadfast sentry: set firmly upon the land, stirring only slightly in the wind, and pointing straight up toward heaven. Most significantly, because its color and vibrancy remain constant throughout the year—even during the coldest, most barren days of winter—it suggests eternal life, and never-ending freshness.

These reasons alone could explain why we bring evergreen trees (or their near equivalents) into our homes at Christmastime and embellish them so lovingly. But in fact, the Christmas tree is the product of over 4,000 years of complex artistic, religious, political, and social input. In every period in recorded history, and in virtually every inhabited region of the globe, trees in general, and evergreen trees in particular, have been the focal point of winter ceremonies honoring the renewal of the natural world, and the refreshing of the human spirit.

Zagmuck in Babylonia: The First Solstice Trees

In Western culture, the tradition of a sacred tree associated with a wintertime holiday can be traced back to the Mesopotamian kingdoms of 2000 B.C. The festival known as Zagmuck in Babylonia lasted twelve days, rounding the end of the old year and the beginning of the new one, just as the twelve-day Christmas holiday—Christmas to Twelfth Night—does today. The reigning Babylonian king was compelled to "re-validate" himself for the new year by doing battle with a challenger: in some cases, a ceremonial mock king; in others, an actual rival.

The annual Zagmuck struggle between kings mirrored the myth of the battle of the Babylonian sun-god Marduk against the force of darkness. The battle took place on the winter solstice, December 21, the

longest night of the year. Trees dedicated to the mythical Marduk, representing the troops he had raised with his life force (sunlight), were erected and decorated prior to the mortal king's battle, and then burned in a bonfire afterwards. The main purpose of this bonfire was to consume a large log, representing the defeated king, that had been cut from the trunk of yet another ceremonial tree.

The Mediterranean Tradition: Ancient Jewish, Greek, and Roman Roots

From the earliest, Mesopotamian point of origin for the Christmas tree, two main traditions can be traced: One is Mediterranean, the other is North European.

The Mediterranean tradition began in the Middle East and then spread westward across the Mediterranean Sea, as the Phoenician, Greek, and Roman empires expanded.

One strand of the Mediterranean winter evergreen tradition involves the Jews. The tree of life in the Garden of Eden is commonly interpreted as an evergreen. The branches and pyramidal shape of this tree are believed to have inspired the shape of the *menorah*, the symbolic Jewish candle holder which figures prominently during Hanukkah, the wintertime feast of lights. Specifically, Hanukkah commemorates a Jewish victory over an enemy; but symbolically, Hanukkah, like other winter solstice holidays before it, also celebrates the victory of light over darkness in the dead of winter.

Another major strand of the Mediterranean tradition involves the ancient Greeks and Romans. Every Greek city-state held a wintertime new year/solstice festival celebrating the defeat of Chronos by Zeus for the title of "father of the gods." Special trees—evergreens as well as other types—were draped in cloths or in garlands of flowers and herbs to honor Zeus, the new-made celestial king.

In later-emerging Roman mythology, Chronos (whom the Romans renamed Saturn) fled to Italy after his defeat by Zeus and inaugurated a golden age in that land. To honor Saturn and to invoke that golden age for every new year, the ancient Romans celebrated a wintertime festival known as Saturnalia.

As long as the Roman Empire lasted, Saturnalia was a highly exuberant holiday of feasting, gift-giving, storytelling, and revelry. Immediately after Saturnalia came the Kalendae festival, honoring the start of the new year. The term Kalendae survives to this day in the words used by Slavic and Baltic peoples to refer to the Christmas season in general: e.g., the Polish Kolenda, the Russian Kolyada, and the Czech Koleda.

All during Saturnalia and Kalendae, homes and public buildings in the Roman Empire were lavishly decorated with evergreen trees and boughs to remind everyone of the upcoming return of greenness to the world. The evergreens themselves were ornamented with candles, gilded berries, and small trinkets to be plucked as gifts. They also bore clay figurines of Bacchus, god of greenery and wine, as the Roman poet Virgil describes in his *Georgics* (Dryden's translation):

> In jolly hymns they praise the god of wine,
> Whose earthen images adorn the pine,
> And those are hung on high in honor of the vine.

The cult of Mithra, the Persian sun god, became dominant within the Roman empire shortly before the advent of Christianity. Mithra was said to have risen from the dead on the winter solstice, thereby promising new life to all who followed him. The Mithraic feast of Brumalia, the birthday of the invincible sun, was incorporated into Saturnalia on December 21, the date of the winter solstice. From then on, the Saturnalian evergreen trees were frequently crowned with small models of Mithra, his head radiating spokes of light.

Christmas Tree Idea

Dress an outside tree for the birds,
with popcorn-and-cranberry strings, suet balls,
and oatmeal raisin cookies.

The North European Yule Festival

During the same era when citizens of the Roman Empire were using evergreens to celebrate Saturnalia, a similar tradition flourished across North Europe. The North European tradition had travelled up the Danube River from the Middle East as successive waves of migratory people made their way deeper and deeper into the greater European woodlands. Indeed, trees in general, especially evergreen trees, were more venerated in North Europe, where they were essential providers of shelter, fuel, and even nourishment, than they were in the warmer and more fertile lands of South Europe.

Whenever a new North European community was founded, the settlers were accustomed to leaving a group of trees—ideally, evergreens—in the center of the main clearing, with one central tree often designated as the mother tree. These trees henceforth functioned as the hub of all social, religious, and political life in the community. They would always be adorned on festive occasions, especially the winter solstice, when everyone in the community desperately needed distraction from the ravages of the severe North European winter.

Among the ancient Celts of present-day France, Great Britain, and Ireland, both oak trees and evergreen trees—and especially one species of evergreen oak—were bedecked at the winter solstice with apples to symbolize fruitfulness, and mistletoe to ward off evil spirits. The same custom was followed by the ancient Teutons of present-day Germany and Scandinavia.

The popular evergreen oak was a reminder that the Oak King, the most revered god among the Celts and Teutons, was a deciduous or dying king for half of the year, and an evergreen or immortal king for the other half of the year. The ancient word for this sacred species is variously spelled *tin, tinne, tannen,* or *glastin.* This root survives in English words like *tanning* (a process of dyeing hides, originally done with oak or pine resin), and the German word *Tannenbaum* for the evergreen fir Christmas tree. It also forms part of the English place name Glastonbury, as in the Glastonbury Thorn, a long-honored variety of hawthorn, first noted on the site of present-day Glastonbury, that often blooms at Christmas time.

Among the ancient Norse, the winter solstice tree (most often evergreen, but sometimes oak) was specifically meant to represent Yggdrasil, the universe-axis world tree that figures in the Norse creation myth, and that is roughly analogous to the Judeo-Christian tree of life. According to Norse mythology, Odin, the father of the gods, hanged himself for nine nights upon the Yggdrasil, an evergreen ash, in order to learn the mysteries of life. In this manner, he brought enlightenment to gods and mortals alike.

Accordingly, the Odin-honoring solstice tree was often encircled with a ring of candles. And the solstice tree was always living: Trees used for indoor decoration were dug up and potted, not cut, so that they could be replanted after the festivities and, in many cases, used again the following year.

Besides a special tree to honor Odin at the winter solstice, there was also a special tree derivative. To symbolize his role as a light-bearer, a particularly thick and long-lasting log, oak if possible, was burned overnight on December 21. Many cultural historians consider this log to be a direct descendent of the log burned during Zagmuck in Babylonia. The ancient Norse holiday was officially known as Yule, from Yolnir, a less familiar name for Odin, and so the special solstice tree was known as a Yule tree, and the special solstice log was known as a Yule log.

The Rise of Christmas and the Fall of Trees

The early Christians in the Roman Empire did not celebrate Christ's birth at all. Even after Christianity was proclaimed the official religion of the empire in the third century A.D., there was no official Christmas. Saturnalia, however, remained popular as a solstice festival— secular on the surface, but still imbued with religious feelings attached to Mithra.

Finally, in 375 A.D., Julius I, Bishop of Rome, established December 25 as the birthday of Christ. This served to link Christ, rather than Mithra, with the winter solstice, and thereby replaced the celebration of Saturnalia with the celebration of Christmas.

In concert with the establishment of Christmas came the appropriation of many of the Saturnalia traditions: feasting, gift-giving, story-telling (especially in the form of carols), and the ceremonial lighting of candles and fires. Strictly forbidden, however, was the use of evergreens as decorations. They were too strongly linked not only with Saturnalia but also with other pagan celebrations that related to the solstice. Nevertheless, the custom of decorating with evergreens around solstice time was never completely eradicated.

As Christianity spread north, where evergreens were far more abundant, this ban on solstice evergreens became more and more troublesome to impose. Ultimately, the Church was forced to find evergreens an acceptable—if not official—place in the Christmas celebration.

The turning point came during Saint Boniface's historic conversion mission among the people of present-day northern Germany during the mid-700s.

Saint Boniface and the First Christmas Tree

The early Germanic campaigns of the English missionary Saint Boniface (also known as Saint Winfred) were highly successful in converting masses of the common people to Christianity. In fact, Saint Boniface was called to Rome to receive special commendation for his work from Pope Gregory II himself.

Nevertheless, Saint Boniface had always had trouble convincing the *rulers* of the Alemanic and Frankish tribes to abandon their old gods and take the Christian God seriously. In fact, when he returned to Germany from Rome at the time of the winter solstice, he discovered that the Alemanic chieftain Gundhar was preparing to sacrifice his eldest son to the god Thor beneath a giant oak tree. In many Teutonic tribes, Thor, rather than Odin, was the focus of solstice worship, and claimed the oak as his sacred tree.

Horrified by what Gundhar intended to do, Saint Boniface decided to take advantage of this occasion to demonstrate that Thor was powerless, thus preventing the sacrifice and furthering his own efforts to convert pagan rulers to Christianity. Just as the grisly ceremony was about to start, Saint Boniface strode up to the oak, pulled out an axe from beneath his robe, and smote the oak with one mighty blow. At that very moment, according to legend, a fierce gust of wind arose and toppled the oak to the ground, revealing a small, young, perfectly shaped fir tree just behind it.

Inspired by this natural symbol of hope and survival, Boniface pointed to the tree and said (as he later recorded):

> This is the word, and this is the message.
> Not a drop of blood shall be shed tonight,
> for this is the birth-night of the Saint
> Christ, Son of the All-Father and Savior of
> the world. This tiny tree, a child of the
> forest, shall be a home tree tonight. It is
> the wood of peace, for your houses are built
> of fir. It is the symbol of endless life, for
> its branches are ever green. See how it
> gestures toward God's heaven! Let this be

called the Christ Child's Tree. Gather about
it, not in the wilderness but in your home.
There it will shelter no bloody deed, but
loving gifts and the lights of kindness.

Saint Boniface also saw to it that the wood from Thor's fallen oak was used in the construction of a monastery and a church dedicated to Saint Peter. Legend claims that the little fir tree itself was taken to Gundhar's great hall and set up there as the first Christmas tree.

The Paradise Tree

Over the next few centuries in Germany and other areas of Europe, the Christmas tree found a role in church-produced paradise plays. These crowd-pleasing plays were staged inside or outside church buildings on December 24, designated in early church calendars as the Day of Adam and Eve. They dramatized the connection between the fall of Adam and Eve, which brought sin and death to humankind, and the redemption offered by Christ (as prophesied in the *Book of Genesis* [3:15]).

The only prop allowed in a paradise play was a fir tree hung with apples, often painted gold, to represent the Tree of Paradise. Precisely how this Tree of Paradise was dramatically related to the two main trees in the Paradise of Eden—the Tree of Life and the Tree of Knowledge— varied from place to place and from drama to drama.

One school of belief held that Adam took an apple from the Tree of Life when he left Eden, and that this stock eventually produced a tree from which Christ plucked the fruit of redemption. Thus the Tree of Paradise, or Christ's tree, was said to derive from the Tree of Life. An alternative school of belief held that Adam had left Eden with an apple from the Tree of Knowledge, also the source of Eve's apple, and that from this stock grew the tree that was cut for Christ's cross. Thus, the Tree of Paradise was said to derive from the Tree of Knowledge. Most often,

however, the Tree of Paradise was taken to represent both the Tree of Life *and* the Tree of Knowledge. As such, it was a properly superior tree for the new paradise promised by Christ.

Whatever the case, communion wafers were added to the decorations on the Tree of Paradise as time went by. Eventually, paradise plays faded away from history, but the tree survived as a Christmas tree—at least in private homes. The apples evolved into Christmas bulbs and the wafers into Christmas cookies.

Martin Luther and the Modern Christmas Tree

By the sixteenth century, the Christmas tree itself seemed in danger of extinction. Its appeal had waned in direct proportion to the increasing demand for more sophisticated, artificial Christmas decorations.

One of the most popular of these new-style decorations was the Christmas pyramid. Although its precise construction varied from region to region, it was essentially a stylized evergreen tree, composed of successively smaller wooden platforms mounted on top of each other and supporting candles, fruits, and various other Christmas-related ornaments (among them, small figurines of Adam, Eve, and the serpent, as well as Mary, Joseph, and the Christ Child). A certain variety of Christmas pyramid had twelve tiers for the twelve days of Christmas, and many authorities believe that the carol "The Twelve Days of Christmas" derives from a decorating scheme for such a pyramid.

The Reformation, however, brought a widespread return to the simpler tradition of a tree at Christmas. Folklore attributes this development personally to Martin Luther, who is known to have been especially fond of Christmas.

As the story goes, Luther was walking home through the woods on a clear, cold Christmas Eve after having delivered a sermon at his church. Stopping in a grove of towering pine trees to admire the stars, he was struck by how much it looked as if the stars were actually hanging in

Lizbeth B. Coming

the branches of the trees. He was also impressed by the trees themselves. Their fragrance seemed far finer to him than the incense he remembered in Roman Catholic churches, and the soft sound made by their branches stirring in the wind suggested a devout congregation at prayer.

Inspired by this experience, Luther cut down a small pine tree and took it home with him. There he filled the branches with small candles, telling his children to imagine that the lit candles were stars in the sky

on the night of Christ's birth. Beneath the tree, he placed small figures of the Holy Family.

Whether or not the story is true, Luther did set up a Christmas tree each year in his home, as did many other Europeans who were intent on returning to more natural and fundamental ways of celebrating Christmas. It's a trend that continues to this day, and has resulted in the era of the modern Christmas tree.

Christmas Tree Idea

Put a small amount of dirt from your garden or your potted plants into the tree water, and the garden or plants will thrive in the coming year.

Milestones in Modern Christmas Tree History

1531   According to records, Christmas trees were sold on a street corner in the Alsatian town of Strasbourg, making this spot the first known Christmas tree market. In fact, there's been a Christmas tree market every year since then in Strasbourg. For the past century, it has dominated the Place Broglie in the very heart of the city. In proud recognition of this history, Strasbourg now calls itself the "Home of the Christmas Tree."

Despite the legend of Martin Luther and the candle-lit Christmas tree, most celebrants in Alsace and other parts of greater Germany during the 1500s kept their Christmas tree bare, being content to admire its fresh green color and pleasing fragrance. Also, an ordinance existed in several Alsatian towns stating that no person "shall have for Christmas more than one bush of more than eight shoe lengths," which at that time meant a tree somewhere around four feet in height. By contrast, Truman Capote wrote in his twentieth century classic, "A Christmas Memory," that a Christmas tree "should be twice as tall as a boy. So a boy can't steal the star."

1605   The earliest record of a modern decorated Christmas tree appeared in a travel diary: "At Christmas, they set up fir trees in the parlors at Strasbourg and hang thereon roses cut from paper of many different colors, apples, wafers, gold foil, sugar sweets, etc." From this entry, we can infer that decorated trees were becoming customary.

[NOTE: For milestones relating to American community trees, such as the Rockefeller Center tree, the White House tree, and the nation's Christmas tree, see the next section of this book, "The Community Christmas Tree."]

c. 1650   In his book *The Milk of the Catechism*, Dr. Johann Dannhauer, a preacher at the Cathedral of Strasbourg, complained about "the Christmas—or fir—tree, which people erect in their houses, hang with dolls and sweets, and afterwards shake and deflower . . . Whence comes the custom, I know not; it is child's play . . . Far better were it to point the children to the spiritual cedar-tree, Jesus Christ."

1708   Liselotte von der Pfalz, sister-in-law of Louis XIV, wrote a letter offering the first description of modern trees decorated with candles (one tree per child, according to common custom): "Tables are fixed up like altars and outfitted for each child with all sorts of things, such as new clothes, silver, dolls, sugar candy, and so forth. Boxwood trees are set on the tables, and a candle is fastened to each branch."

1776   According to an unsubstantiated story, when George Washington and his troops attacked Trenton, New Jersey, on Christmas night, they surprised Hessian (German) mercenaries celebrating around a candle-lit Christmas tree. Whether or not this story is true, it is known that Hessians serving with the British in the Revolutionary War introduced candle-lit Christmas trees to the children of Newport, Rhode Island.

1804   A captain in the U.S. Army set up a Christmas tree at Fort Dearborn, Michigan. He claimed to have picked up the custom from the Hessians during the Revolutionary War.

1823   A curious public notice appeared in the York, Pennsylvania *Gazette*, written by an organization entitled the "Society of Bachelors" and describing an upcoming meeting: "The Old Maids have determined to present us with at least one Cart of Ginger-cakes, the society in turn therefore intend fixing *Krischkintle Bauhm* [in Pennsylvania Dutch, "Christ Child Tree," or "Kriss Kringle Tree"] for the amusement of such as may think proper to give them a call. Its decorations shall be superb, superfine, superfrostical, shnockagastical, double refined, mill' twill'd made of Dog's Wool, Swingling Tow, and Posnum fur; which cannot fail to gratify taste."

1830   In the first recorded use of a Christmas tree in a fund-raising context, the Dorcas Society of York, Pennsylvania, a group of women interested in clothing poor widows and orphans, charged 6½¢ to view a decorated Christmas tree.

1832   Charles Follen, a political refugee from Germany teaching German at Harvard College, decorated a tree for his son in Boston, Massachusetts, and allowed many friends and prominent Bostonians to view it. Because of the interest that it generated among prominent citizens who had never heard of a Christmas tree before, it is considered in many accounts to be the first American Christmas tree.

The decorations on the Follen tree included baskets of sugar plums, gilded egg cups, paper cornucopias filled with sweets, tiny dolls, assorted "whimsies," and a wax taper on every branch. The overall effect when the tapers were lit was so impressive that one observer was quoted as saying, "I have little doubt the Christmas tree will become one of the most flourishing exotics of New England."

1842 Charles Minnigerode, an emigrant from Germany teaching at the College of William and Mary in Virginia, decorated a Christmas tree for the children of his friend Judge Tucker with strings of popcorn and gilded nuts. Tucker continued to erect a tree each year thereafter; and today, at Williamsburg, a community tree is set up at Christmas outside of the Tucker home.

Christmas Tree Idea

Decorate the tree according to the items mentioned in the poem/song, "The Twelve Days of Christmas" (which, in fact, refers to Christmas tree decorations).

1845 The artist C. A. Schwerdgeburth painted a picture of Martin Luther and his family seated around a candle-bearing Christmas tree. This picture was reproduced and distributed throughout Europe and the United States, doing much to perpetuate the legend that Martin Luther "invented" the candle-bearing Christmas tree, and to advance the popularity of Christmas trees in general.

1847 August Ingard, a German-born tailor, decorated a Christmas tree for his nieces and nephews in Wooster, Ohio.

The novel tree so charmed the people of Wooster that they encouraged Ingard to exhibit such a tree every Christmas afterwards. Today, in honor of this tradition, a decorated tree is placed at his tomb in Wooster during each Christmas season.

1848   The *Illustrated London News* published a cover drawing of Queen Victoria, Prince Albert, and their children gathered around a Christmas tree. It attracted an overwhelming amount of interest, doing more than anything else to legitimize the Christmas tree, and to establish it as an integral part of future Christmas festivities throughout Britain and the Western world.

In fact, Prince Albert, who was born and raised in Germany, had added a Christmas tree to the British royal celebration of Christmas eight years earlier, in 1840. Given the Victorian era's emphasis on family togetherness, and its nostalgia for the medieval world, there's little wonder that the domestic Christmas tree quickly became so popular.

1850   *Godey's Lady's Book*, a popular periodical in America, printed the same drawing of the British royal family around the Christmas tree that was used in the 1848 *Illustrated London News*. The American version omitted Queen Victoria's distinctive tiara and left the royal family unidentified as such. However, the effect was the same: an immediate, widespread, and lasting enthusiasm for decorated trees at Christmas time.

1851   Mike Carr, a farmer living in the Catskill Mountains of upstate New York, started the first recorded Christmas tree business in the United States. In early December, he shipped trees by steamboat to New York City and set them up in Washington Market, a wholesale food and vegetable outlet centered around present-day Greenwich Street and extending west to the Hudson River.

By the 1880s, there were over 600 separate tree dealers competing for space in the Washington Market, bringing with them almost a quarter million trees from all over the Northeast. Some dealers were forced to sell their trees right off the decks of their ships. Because of the competition, prices were quite low. A small tree sold for about 10 cents; a large one (8-10 feet tall) for about a quarter.

1851   Reverend Henry Schwan set up a Christmas tree in his church in Cleveland, Ohio. Many members of the congregation complained about the tree's "paganism" and forced him to take it down. Hearing of the controversy, another Cleveland pastor sympathetic to Schwan sent a Christmas tree to Schwan's church as a gift. No one in the congregation was willing to object to a Christmas gift, and so the tree was installed. In succeeding years, a gift tree always appeared at the church at Christmastime.

1854   Charles Dickens published a description of a Christmas tree in an article for the magazine *Household Words*, not only enhancing the Christmas tree's popularity, but also inspiring tree decorators to be more imaginative:

> *"I have been looking on, this evening, at a merry company of children assembled around that pretty German toy, a Christmas tree. The tree was planted in the middle of a great*

round table, and towered high above their heads. It was brilliantly lighted by a multitude of little tapers; and everywhere sparkled and glittered with bright objects. There were rosy-cheeked dolls, hiding behind green leaves; and there were real watches . . . dangling from innumerable twigs; there were French polished tables, chairs, bedsteads, wardrobes, eight-day clocks, and various other articles of domestic furniture (wonderfully made in tin) perched among the boughs, as if in preparation for some fairy housekeeping; there were jolly, broad-faced little men, much more agreeable in appearance than many real men—and no wonder, for their heads took off, and showed them to be full of sugar-plums. . . . This motley collection of odd objects, clustering on the tree like magic fruit . . . set me thinking how all the trees that grow and all the things that come into existence on the earth, have their wild adornments at that well remembered time."

1862 References were made in San Francisco newspapers to Christmas trees—the first evidence that the custom of erecting Christmas trees had reached the West Coast.

1878 A New York reporter, alarmed at the popularity of the pagan Christmas tree, called it an "aboriginal oddity."

1882 Edward Johnson, a colleague of Thomas Edison, displayed the first electrically lit Christmas tree. As reported in the *Detroit Post and Tribune*:

"It was brilliantly lighted with many colored globes about as large as an English walnut and was turning some six times a *minute on a little pine box. There were 80 lights in all encased in these dainty glass eggs, and about equally divided between white, red, and blue. As the tree turned, the colors alternated, all the lamps going out and being relit at every revolution. . . . I need not tell you that the scintillating evergreen was a pretty sight—one can hardly imagine anything prettier."*

Well into the 1890s, installing electric lights on a Christmas tree was an expensive proposition. Bulbs were not attached to strings, but were sold individually on separate wires for about a dollar each. Assuming thirty lights were installed, the bill for electricity service could easily total $100—a very high cost in those days.

The *New York Times* sharply attacked this "wasteful" practice, stating, "The little children of the rich have grown critical with overabundance, and nothing short of an electric tree, with fairy effects produced by the wizard bower, satisfies them." Fortunately, far more economical strings of lights began appearing in the marketplace shortly after the turn of the century.

1883 The editor of the *New York Times*, a devout churchman, bewailed the candle-lit Christmas tree in print as a "rootless and lifeless corpse—never worthy of the day" and predicted that educated people would soon tire of the custom:

"The Christmas tree, dropping melted wax upon the carpet, filling all nervous people with a dread of fire . . . diffusing the poison of rationalism thinly disguised as the perfume of hemlock, should have no place in our beloved land."

1897 According to a widely published news story, James Clements, a former railroad brakeman who struck it rich in the Klondike gold rush, decorated a Christmas tree in his New York City hotel room with $70,000 worth of gold nuggets.

1900 The U.S. Forest Service reported that one in every five American households erected and decorated an evergreen tree indoors at Christmastime. Thirty years later, the Forest Service reported that the Christmas tree was nearly universal among American households.

1906 The German kaiser displayed twelve lavishly decorated Christmas trees, varying in size according to the size of the tree's recipient: one for himself, one for his wife, six for his sons, three for his daughters, and one for his grandchild. The trees were mounted on tables, at this time still the prevailing custom for Christmas trees everywhere; but the floor-mounted tree soon became the tree of choice.

1914 According to a *New York Times* article, Valentine Williams, a captain of the Irish Guard, witnessed a heartwarming Christmas Eve scene on a World War I battleground:

> *"Gray figures from the German trenches came over to the English line with little Christmas trees, and cried in broken English, 'Merry Christmas, Tommy!' That Christmas Eve, lighted Christmas trees formed a chain of light all along the endless German line of communications from the front line in France to German headquarters. Before anybody realized*

what was happening, men from the trenches on either side were scrambling into No-Man's Land, laughing, cheering, singing. Then rifles were laid aside, hands were clasped in Christmas friendship, cigars and cigarettes handed out, and gifts exchanged. The Germans sang, 'Stille Nacht, Heilige Nacht [Silent Night]' and 'O Tannenbaum,' and the English responded with 'Good King Wenceslas.'"

Christmas Tree Idea

When you are about to discard your tree, cut off a section of the trunk, burn it, and spread the ashes on your garden or in your potted plants. Or save the trunk section to burn as next year's yule log.

The Community
Christmas Tree

According to Greek mythology, the Titan Prometheus took fire from heaven and gave it to humankind. Executed in bronze and covered with gold leaf, this landmark statue of Prometheus is a permanent fixture of Rockefeller Center and serves as an appropriate guardian of the Rockefeller Center Christmas Tree.

he United States of America has made many contributions to the modern history of the Christmas tree, including the floor-length tree (as opposed to the tabletop tree), electric tree lights, mass-produced Christmas tree bulbs, and specialized Christmas tree farms. The most significant contribution, however, has been the concept of the community Christmas tree.

The community tree concept itself dates back to antiquity, when ancient, forest-bound villages would leave, plant, or erect a centrally located tree to serve as the focal point for community celebrations, including winter solstice festivities. But the concept died out during the Middle Ages, as Europe became increasingly Christian and civilized. It took the vital spirit of a new nation of settlements, not far removed from their forest-bound origins and still developing their own sense of community, to revitalize that concept in the form of a Christmas tree.

By definition, a community Christmas tree is any Christmas tree that belongs to the public, as opposed to a particular household, church, or business establishment. The tree might be live or cut, indoors or outdoors. It might be decorated traditionally, as most trees are, to reflect prevailing tastes. Or it might be decorated to convey a special theme—perhaps the community's heritage—or to serve a special purpose, such as the recent trend toward trimming trees with mittens, muffs, caps, and scarves for homeless people. And the public that it serves might be a neighborhood, a town, a city, or even the entire country.

The most famous community Christmas trees that belong to the United States as a whole are the White House tree in Washington, D.C., the Rockefeller Center tree in New York City, and the Nation's Christmas tree in King's Canyon National Park, California. These trees are discussed separately in this section of the book. Here is a timetable of major events involving other, more localized community Christmas tree traditions.

1909 Residents of Pasadena, California, decorated a large evergreen tree atop Mount Wilson with electric lights, creating the first known outdoor community Christmas tree in America—

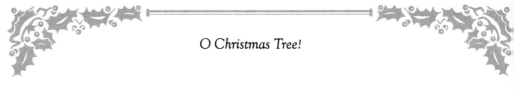

or, for that matter, in the entire world—since at least the Reformation (sixteenth century). Throughout the Christmas season, the Pasadena tree was visible all over the city.

1911 A community Christmas tree, the Tree of Light, was set up in Madison Square Garden in New York City, near 25th Street and Fifth Avenue. It was a 60-foot balsam fir. The first such tree on the East Coast, it attracted a crowd of over 20,000 on the night it was lit. Two years later, another community tree was set up at City Hall.

1912 In Boston, a lavish display of Christmas lights, including decorated evergreens, was mounted in the Commons.

1913 Philadelphia erected a 75-foot spruce tree, "The Children's Christmas Tree," in Independence Square, the start of an ongoing tradition.

1920 Altadena, California (uphill from Pasadena) inaugurated its mile-long "Christmas Tree Lane," a road flanked by 200 deodar cedars decorated with over 10,000 multicolored lights. The cedars were planted there in 1882 by Frederick J. Woodbury, who brought them back from India himself. At that time, the road was just a trail on Woodbury's ranch, not an actual town street.

1921 The Horse's Christmas Tree was established in Boston's Post Office Square by the Society for the Prevention of

Cruelty to Animals. It was thickly bedecked with apples, sugar lumps, and doughnuts intended to serve as Christmas treats for the many draft animals working in that area. The practice continued throughout the 1920s.

1930   Bethlehem, Pennsylvania, founded in the eighteenth century by immigrant members of the Moravian Church (a Protestant sect originating in the Moravian area of Czechoslovakia), began institutionalizing a citywide Christmas celebration. By this time, the Moravians had long been famous throughout Pennsylvania for their love of Christmas in general and Christmas trees in particular.

The festivities have evolved since 1930 to include an elaborate display of 150 community spruce trees lit by 1,200 electric lights spanning Bethlehem's Hill-to-Hill Bridge, crowned in the center by a 60-foot tree made up of smaller trees. Also, a giant Electric Star of Bethlehem has been erected on the summit of nearby South Mountain. Bethlehem's continuing tradition of celebrating Christmas so exuberantly has earned it the title, The Christmas City of America.

1940   In Wilmington, North Carolina, a majestic live oak draped in Spanish moss was illuminated for Christmas.

1947   Minneapolis, Minnesota, created a 65-foot-tall community Christmas tree by attaching water pipe branches to a telephone pole, and then covering these branches with a total of 135 small evergreen trees.

1948 A 96-foot white spruce Christmas tree was set up in Pershing Square, Los Angeles. Also, a 134-foot Douglas fir was set up in Bellingham, Washington.

1950 Northgate Shopping Center near Seattle, Washington, erected the tallest community Christmas tree on record: a 221-foot fir weighing 25 tons and sporting more than 3,000 electric lights. This record still stands.

Christmas Tree Idea

Place mistletoe at the top of the tree. Thereafter, any small branch of the tree that you cut off is a love charm. Place the piece under your pillow and you'll dream of your love. Place it in someone's pocket and that person will be induced to love you.

The Rockefeller Center
Christmas Tree

Christmas in New York City would not be the same without the Rockefeller Center Christmas tree. And, thanks to nationwide media services (many of which have their national headquarters in the Rockefeller Center area), neither would Christmas in America.

The Rockefeller Center Christmas tree has turned into a beloved institution as closely associated with the U.S.A. in general as the World Series, Disneyland, or Old Faithful. Here are some milestones in its proud and colorful history:

1931 **W**orkmen involved in the construction of Rockefeller Center set up a 20-foot tree of their own, decorated with strands of tinsel, on the mud-covered future site of the Channel Gardens. It was admired by onlookers who could see it over—and through—the fence surrounding the block. On Christmas Eve, the workmen received their pay beside this tree.

1933 **T**o celebrate the opening of the 70-story RCA Building, the management took a cue from the workmen and formally started the Rockefeller Center Christmas tree tradition. They erected a tree trimmed with 700 blue and white lights on the sidewalk in front of the building. Christmas music was furnished by choirs from local churches and Columbia University (whose campus formerly occupied the site).

On Christmas Eve 1931, workmen constructing the RCA Building gather next to their own, private tree to receive their holiday paychecks. Little do they realize that a tree close to the same spot in Rockefeller Center will soon become an annual public Christmas spectacle.

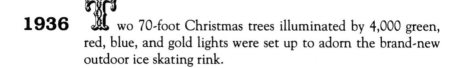

1936 Two 70-foot Christmas trees illuminated by 4,000 green, red, blue, and gold lights were set up to adorn the brand-new outdoor ice skating rink.

1941 Two live reindeer from the Bronx Zoo were housed in cages on either side of the tree. In addition to lighting the tree, there had been plans to light an electric candle in each window of the RCA Building. However, the advent of World War II imposed blackout restrictions that wouldn't permit such a lavish display. Permission was granted to light the tree itself, but it remained dark for the next three years.

1945 Celebrating the end of World War II and the blackout, the tree was lit in an extraordinary way: with fluorescent plastic globes that glowed when a black light was focused on them.

1948 The tallest Rockefeller Center Christmas tree in all the years before or since was erected: a 90-foot Norway spruce, decorated with 600 white plastic globes, 600 white plastic snowflakes, and 7,500 gold and silver electric lights. The average tree over the years has been about 60 feet tall.

1949 The tree was spray painted with several hundred gallons of silvery paint, then covered with 500 plastic globes and 7,500 lights in brilliant carnival colors of blue, yellow, orange, and red.

1950 The tree was decorated with a half-mile chain of 3,600 white and red balls, designed to look like a giant garland of popcorn and cranberries. In the Channel Gardens across the ice rink from the tree, a blanket of stars was hung from a grid-work of 54 cross cables to represent the heavens as they appeared in this area at 9 P.M. Christmas Eve.

1951 The tree lighting was broadcast on television coast-to-coast for the first time, as part of the "Kate Smith Show." Later, it served as the background for the nationally televised "Lucky Strike Hit Parade," which staged its Christmas show in Rockefeller Plaza.

1966 Canada gave Rockefeller Center its first—and, so far, only—tree from outside the United States, in honor of the centennial of Canada's confederation. Thus, the Rockefeller Center Christmas tree this year was a community tree not just for the United States, but for Canada as well.

1970 Twelve gigantic wire-sculpted angels were set up in the Channel Gardens to herald the tree, lit by 10,000 lights. The angels have since become a traditional feature.

1971 For the first time, the tree was recycled after the Christmas season. The mulch was presented to the New York City Department of Parks for use on the nature trails in Inwood Hill Park in Manhattan. Since then, the tree mulch has been donated each year to different groups in various parts of the country.

Trumpeting angels line the Channel Gardens leading to Rockefeller Center's ice-skating rink and Christmas tree. Fashioned from wire and twinkling lights, the 12-foot-tall angels first heralded the Christmas tree in 1969.

1973 When the 1973 oil crisis threatened to darken the tree—or so it was reported in many news items—people around the country protested. One man suggested that a treadmill be set up on a nearby sidewalk to power a generator, so that passing pedestrians could make the tree shine as usual. In fact, the tree was lit according to the original plans, with its by-now-customary 10,000 lights.

1989 Six gigantic wooden cadets were added to the esplanade below the tree and around the rink. They have continued in succeeding years to guard the tree.

Christmas Tree Idea

Place a ring of candles around the tree for
making wishes on Christmas Eve.

The White House
Christmas Tree

Because the White House is the first home of the land, its Christmas tree generates special interest. Thousands of tourists in Washington, D.C., during the Christmas season pass through the Blue Room to admire the tree—which is, after all, their community tree, as opposed to the private tree (or trees) in the White House living quarters. Millions more see the White House Christmas tree on television, in magazines, and in newspapers.

For almost half of our nation's history, there was no Christmas tree in the White House—public or private. Indeed, there was very little celebration of Christmas at all, either in the White House or in the United States.

A significant number of our founding fathers and mothers, as well as their descendents, frowned on Christmas revelry because of its pagan associations, preferring instead to focus on more somber Lenten and Easter observances. The Puritans formally banned Christmas celebrations in early New England. Christmas Day wasn't even a legal holiday anywhere in the United States until 1836, when Alabama finally declared it one. And as late as 1870, public schools in Boston, Massachusetts, remained open as usual on Christmas Day, punishing any students who failed to attend, unless they were sick.

In 1856, President Franklin Pierce and his wife set up a Christmas tree in the White House for the first time. They also invited the entire Sunday School of the New York Avenue Presbyterian Church to view the tree. But the Pierce tree was strictly a family tree. The institution of an official White House Christmas tree didn't actually begin until 1889, with President Benjamin Harrison.

On that Christmas Eve, four generations of Harrisons gathered to enjoy a tree trimmed with candles, silver ornaments, and toys (gifts for the children). The event was well-publicized across the United States. Harrison took advantage of this opportunity to state that "we should make merry for children at Christmastime," and that he hoped his example of erecting "an old-fashioned Christmas tree would be followed by every family in the land."

Here are other significant milestones in the history of the White House Christmas tree:

1895   Grover Cleveland was the first president to use electric lights on the tree. Hand-blown light bulbs, resembling dainty eggs, had to be wired and attached individually to each branch by an electrician.

President Benjamin Harrison could have had his 1889 tree electrified, but he was notoriously afraid of electricity. He and his wife refused to touch the newly installed electric light switches in the White House. Servants did this for them.

1900   Alarmed by U.S. Forest Service reports of declining timber acreage in America, President Theodore Roosevelt, an ardent conservationist, announced that there would be no White House Christmas tree while he was president.

1901   Theodore Roosevelt's sons, Archie and Quentin, smuggled a Christmas tree into Archie's closet and decorated it as a treat for their parents on Christmas Day. When Roosevelt saw it, he lectured his sons about conservation and sent them to talk with cabinet member Gifford Pinchot, America's first professional forester. To Roosevelt's surprise, Pinchot advised

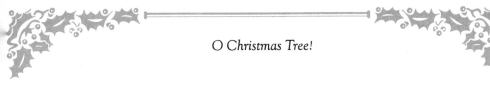

them to tell their father that properly managed Christmas tree cutting could actually benefit forests by thinning them.

Each succeeding Christmas that Roosevelt remained in the White House, he informed the press that there would be no official presidential tree. Archie, however, was granted permission to set up a small, private tree in his own room.

1923 Having received a gift Christmas tree from his native Vermont, President Calvin Coolidge decorated it outdoors, on the White House grounds, so that more people could enjoy it. This move began the tradition of an outdoor community tree as well as an indoor community tree.

The outdoor tree became popularly known as the Nation's Christmas Tree (not to be confused with the General Grant Tree in King's Canyon National Park, California, which now bears the same title). The indoor tree has continued to be known as the White House Christmas Tree.

1940 For the first time, glass Christmas tree ornaments did not have to be imported from Germany (which was now cut off from trade by World War II). Instead, they were available from an American manufacturer, Corning. President Franklin D. Roosevelt used such ornaments to decorate the White House Christmas tree.

Unlike his presidential uncle Theodore, Franklin had a passion for Christmas trees. He actually helped popularize the idea of growing Christmas trees by planting thousands of spruces on the grounds of his own estate in Hyde Park, New York and then marketing the grown specimens. Whenever he voted, he gave "Christmas tree farmer" as his occupation.

1959 In addition to the official White House tree, President Dwight D. Eisenhower and his wife set up twenty-five other trees throughout the public and private sections of the mansion, a record that still stands. Surprisingly, some of the decorations used on the trees were gifts sent by Nikita Khrushchev, premier of the Soviet Union and, officially, an atheist.

1961 President John F. Kennedy's wife Jacqueline decorated the White House Christmas tree with ornaments suggesting Tchaikowsky's *Nutcracker* ballet: sugarplum fairies, candy canes, toy musical instruments, lollipops, toy soldiers, imitation mice, and miniature baskets of fruit. It started a trend among first ladies of always choosing a special theme for the tree.

1966 For the first time, the White House Christmas tree was provided by the National Christmas Tree Association (NCTA), a professional group made up of people involved in the production and sale of real Christmas trees and related industry services. The tree itself was chosen through state and national competition (won in 1966 by a farmer from Black River Falls, Wisconsin). The NCTA has provided the White House Christmas tree every year since, and it has always been chosen in the same manner.

Have A Real Tree
Merry Christmas

SM

The logo of the National Christmas Tree Association (NCTA) bids Americans to celebrate Christmas with a live tree, rather than an artificial one, which is precisely what most Americans do—including the nation's President. Every year since 1966, the NCTA, representing tree growers and marketers across the nation, has provided the White House Christmas tree. For more information about this environmentally active organization, contact NCTA, 611 East Wells Street, Milwaukee, WI 53202, (414) 276-6410.

The Nation's Christmas Tree

sked to imagine a Christmas tree, most people visualize a slender, pyramidal fir or pine tree, cut and decorated, whose bottom branches hover inches from the ground, and whose crown extends about 4, 8, 16, 32, or, possibly, even 64 feet into the air. The official Nation's Christmas Tree looks nothing like this!

Instead, the Nation's Christmas tree is a living tree, not a cut tree, that remains undecorated for the entire year, including Christmastime. More to the point, it is not a fir tree or a pine tree at all, but a giant sequoia. It towers 267.4 feet tall, with its lowest branch hanging about 100 feet above ground level; and it measures a stout 107.5 feet in circumference at the base. Furthermore, it's not pyramidal in shape, or even symmetrical, but rounded off at the top and full of snag injuries, like most ancient sequoias.

The everyday name of the Nation's Christmas tree is the General Grant Tree, after General (and President) Ulysses S. Grant. And its home is the King's Canyon National Park on the north coast of California, where it is one of the most renowned redwoods in seventy-five protected groves scattered along the western slope of the Sierra Nevada Mountains.

Here are major highlights in the remarkable history of our official national Christmas tree:

c. 215 B.C. he tree started growing from seed, about the same time as the Chinese were building their Great Wall to ward off invaders, and Hannibal was crossing the Alps with his elephants to invade Rome. This makes the present-day tree approximately 2,200 years old.

The naturalist John Muir called the sequoia "nature's forest masterpiece, and so far as I know, the greatest of all living things." This sequoia in Kings Canyon National Park, California, is magnificent enough to have earned the title of the Nation's Christmas Tree.

1 A.D. Jesus was born on the first Christmas Day, by which time the tree had achieved about one sixth of its eventual height.

1862 The tree was first seen by American settlers. It was especially striking to them because of its setting: a clearing ringed by much smaller firs, pines, and cedars.

1890 Threatened by logging operations based in Sanger, California (about forty miles away), the tree was protected when the federal government created General Grant National Park, later expanded to become King's Canyon National Park. These very same logging operations were a major catalyst for the American conservation movement in general.

1924 Charles E. Lee of Sanger, California, visited General Grant National Park to see the tree. A little girl beside him exclaimed, "What a wonderful Christmas tree it would make!" The idea stayed with Lee.

1925 Lee convinced the Sanger Chamber of Commerce to hold the first Christmas program of music and prayers beneath the tree, at noon on Christmas Day.

1926 Responding to a campaign launched by Lee, President Calvin Coolidge officially designated the tree the Nation's Christmas tree on April 28.

1956 The tree was also officially proclaimed a national shrine, in honor of men and women who have given their lives in the service of their country. It thus became—and remains—the nation's only living national shrine. The proclamation was delivered by Fleet Admiral Chester Nimitz, representing President Eisenhower.

1976 To commemorate the 50th anniversary of the tree's designation as the Nation's Christmas tree, a special ceremony was held on Christmas Day featuring people who had attended the very first such ceremony in 1926. Annual ceremonies featuring music and prayer are still held beneath the tree on Christmas Day, attracting about 1,000 celebrants each year.

Christmas Tree Idea

Shear the trunk of a discarded Christmas tree and erect it as a maypole the following May 1.

Christmas Tree Stories and Legends

ike celebrating Christmas, storytelling refreshes the human spirit, stretching its capacity to feel and wonder and believe. Hence, Christmastime storytelling is especially magical.

This section of the book tells you twelve stories relating to Christmas trees, one for each of the twelve days of Christmas. Some of them are factual, some of them are fanciful, some of them are part fact and part fancy. But all of them are true, in the sense that they speak clearly, knowledgeably, and accurately about the human spirit. Let them speak to you at Christmastime, and allow yourself the joy of telling them to others!

Also, remember that a vital part of storytelling is creating your own stories. Think of Christmases in your past, and the trees that represented them. Or imagine all the types of Christmas trees there might be, and all the things that might happen—to them, around them, and because of them. Then share your thoughts and imaginative visions with those you love.

The Gift of the Christmas Tree

a German legend

❄   ❄   ❄

Long, long ago, in a remote mountain wood, in a tiny little cabin, there lived a poor forester, his wife, and their two children. All of them worked tirelessly from sunup to sundown. The forester chopped trees into logs, and logs into lumber. His wife tended their garden, scrubbed their cabin, mended their clothes, made soap and candles, and cooked their meager meals. Their two children did whatever they could to help their mother and their father. They were all grateful to God for each other. It was a hard life, but it was a loving one.

Then came a winter storm that was worse than any winter storm had ever been in those parts. Day after day, the forester and his family huddled in their cabin to keep warm, parcelling out small amounts of food each mealtime so that their stock would not run out before the storm did. At night, they gathered together in the same big bed, and told marvelous stories to each other for hours while the wind howled, so that their spirits would not give up before the storm did, and so that they would fall asleep with hope and joy in their hearts.

One night, they heard a rapping on the door. Imagine the forester's surprise when he opened the door and saw a little boy, all covered in dirt and rags! "May I pass the night with you?" the child asked.

The forester didn't hesitate a moment. "You certainly may, little man. How did you come to be wandering outside on such a foul night?" But the little boy didn't answer, and, seeing his sad little eyes, the forester dropped the matter.

His wife led the boy to the hearth fire, undressed him, and bathed him gently and thoroughly, using up a great deal of their precious water supply. Then she gave him clean clothes to wear and sat him down at

their table. "We shall have a special meal to celebrate your being with us tonight, and out of the storm," she said. And so they did, using up a great deal of their food supply. After dinner, the children played with the boy until he was very sleepy, and then the family invited him into their bed to hear their tales, and to sleep warmly and securely in their arms.

The next morning, the forester, his wife, and his children were all awakened at once by the sound of heavenly singing, and by a dazzling white such as they had never seen before. Rushing outside, they saw the little boy standing before them, now radiant. They knew at once that their little lost guest was, in truth, the Christ Child, and they fell to their knees at his feet.

"For your great kindness," said the Christ Child, bidding them to rise, "there is nothing I can bestow upon you that you do not already possess. But let me give you something in remembrance of my visit." He plucked a branch from a nearby fir tree and planted it beside the door to the tiny cabin.

Immediately, the branch grew into a tree, blossomed, and bore all sorts of wondrous fruits. "Behold my gift to you," he said. "This tree shall be my token, and it shall bear fruits for you each year at Christmastime, so that you shall never go hungry."

Such is the story of the first Christbaum, or Christmas tree. Today, its fruit is the promise of life eternal, and the hunger it satisfies is the hunger for redemption.

The Story of Saint Dasius

a Bulgarian legend

✳   ✳   ✳

In the year 303 A.D., Christianity was not yet a universally accepted religion within the Roman Empire. Many citizens—especially soldiers—still honored the old gods, at least on their traditional holidays.

The most popular of these holiday festivities was Saturnalia. A winter solstice feast named for Saturn, father of the Roman gods, Saturnalia also paid homage to Mithra, the Persian sun god, who had allegedly died and then been reborn, promising new life to his believers. Soldiers in the eastern regions of the empire—not far from Persia itself—were especially drawn to Mithra.

At this time, Dasius was a Christian soldier attached to the garrison of Dirostorum, which is known today as Silistra, Bulgaria, a town that lies close to where the Danube meets the Black Sea. As Saturnalia approached, he was determined to withdraw from the general company as much as he could, so that he could remain true to his Christian beliefs. Fate had other plans.

Each Saturnalia, as the legend goes, it was the custom for the soldiers to draw lots to see who would be the Saturnine "king of the revel." Whoever drew the winning lot would be royally feasted and indulged for thirty days, right up to the winter solstice itself. On that night, December 21, he had to stand upon the Saturnalia altar and kill himself. In the year 303, Dasius drew the winning lot.

As a true Roman soldier, Dasius was not concerned about the death part of the ritual, but he immediately announced his refusal to play a pagan god, no matter how royally he might be treated for his reigning month. The other soldiers argued with him, tortured him, and even threatened him with an instant, very painful death, but he continued to refuse. Finally, they beheaded him.

The story goes that the first blood springing from Dasius's neck nourished a pine cone on the ground. In time, as the empire became more and more Christianized, this pinecone grew into a majestic pine tree. But when the pine tree itself was cut by a soldier looking for firewood, a strange thing happened: Instead of the clear liquid sap that pines had always produced, this pine gave out a thick, sticky sap—almost like blood itself!

An old-timer remembered that it was on this very spot that Dasius had been beheaded, and pronounced the blood-fed pine to be a Christian tree, bleeding for the world's sins as Dasius and Christ before him had bled. Since that time, all pines have produced the same blood-like sap, and so the pine has a special significance at Christmas time.

Whether or not the story of Dasius explains the viscous sap of pine trees, Dasius himself is recognized as a Christian martyr for standing up to pagan soldiers. His sarcophagus can still be visited in Ancona, Bulgaria.

The Glastonbury Thorn

an English legend

❄ ❄ ❄

One of the most compelling and enigmatic symbols associated with early English Christianity is the Holy Grail. In some traditional accounts, the Grail is alleged to be the cup that Jesus used at the Last Supper, when he bade his disciples to drink of his blood. In other accounts, the Grail is described as a cup that collected blood from Jesus's wounds as he suffered on the cross. Common to all accounts is the figure of Joseph of Arimathaea, who gave Jesus's body a tomb, and who is said to have carried the Grail from Jerusalem to England, thereby spreading Christianity through much of western Europe.

A few centuries after the Holy Grail reached England, it was mysteriously lost. Its recovery became the ongoing quest of King Arthur and his Knights of the Round Table. In Arthurian and post-Arthurian sagas, the Grail itself is portrayed both literally, as a chalice, and figuratively, as divine grace.

It so happens that Joseph of Arimathaea's Grail-bearing mission to England is connected with another, similarly evocative symbol—a miraculous Christmas tree, known to history as the Glastonbury Thorn. In strictly religious terms, the Glastonbury Thorn gives the hawthorn tree just as valid a claim to the title of Christmas Tree as the evergreen tree has.

According to tradition, the moment that Joseph of Arimathaea and his twelve companions landed in England with the Holy Grail, they began marching inland. Joseph himself walked with the aid of a hawthorn staff that he had brought all the way from the Holy Land. On Christmas Day, the tired missionaries decided to rest on a hill (now called Weary-All Hill) near Glastonbury, Somerset: the Isle of Avalon in

King Arthur stories. When they reached the top of the hill, Joseph stuck his staff into the ground and—wonder of wonders—it immediately rooted, budded, and blossomed! Thereafter, according to legend, the Glastonbury Thorn bloomed each and every Christmas Day, attracting pilgrims from all over England to the church that Joseph consecrated on that very hill.

In fact, an ancient hawthorn tree was discovered on Weary-All Hill in the fourteenth century, while a chapel was being built there to cover the presumed gravesite of Joseph of Arimathaea. Previously, a church had occupied this same site for an unknown period of time, but it had evidently burned to the ground sometime in the twelfth century. Just as the legend stated, the ancient hawthorn tree actually did produce green leaves every Christmas Day after its discovery!

The renowned Glastonbury Thorn thrived well into the 1600s. Then, the huge, sprawling tree was attacked by a Puritan enraged over the annual veneration bestowed upon it. Before he could completely destroy it with his axe, a large splinter flew into his eye and pierced his brain, killing him on the spot. A small portion of the tree lived on for another thirty years, during which time various thorns were budded from it to produce new trees, not only at Glastonbury itself, but also at other locations throughout England. The Christmas Day blooming continued in this second generation of trees, which were generically called Glastonbury thorns.

When the "new style" calendar was adopted in 1752, making Christmas fall twelve days earlier that year, 2,000 people gathered around a scion of the original Glastonbury Thorn in Quainton, Buckinghamshire on the new December 25. They were eager to see if the tree would blossom and, by doing so, honor the change in calendar. The tree failed to blossom. Therefore, many of those assembled, as well as others who heard about the failure, refused to accept that day as the true Christmas. The Glastonbury Thorn at nearby Glastonbury itself also did not bloom that day, but it *did* bloom on January 5, 1753: the "old style" Christmas Day and the "new style" Twelfth Night.

In 1902, a descendant sprig of the Glastonbury Thorn was presented to the National Cathedral in Washington, D.C., by Stanley Austin, then poet laureate of England. It was planted on Washington's Mount St. Alban even before the ground was broken for the cathedral building. On Christmas Day 1918, it blossomed at Christmas for the first time—a miracle many observers attributed to the recent end of World War I. Since then, it has blossomed only a few times precisely on December 25, but it maintains its reputation as a sacred tree.

Horticulturalists point out that hawthorn trees in general often go through a second annual bloom cycle around Christmastime, depending on various local weather factors during the previous year. This natural tendency alone, however, does not explain the incredible regularity with which the original Glastonbury Thorn blossomed on Christmas Day, nor the incredible regularity with which many of its descendents continue to blossom on Christmas Day. And whether or not one accepts the Christmas blooming of a Glastonbury Thorn as literal evidence of Christian redemption, it offers a powerful symbolic image of new life conquering the death of winter.

The Holly Tree's Penance

an early Christian legend

❄ ❄ ❄

A hardy plant that maintains attractive green or varicolored leaves and red berries throughout the winter months, holly has had a long history of contributing to end-of-the-year celebrations. The ancient Romans (to whom holly represented masculinity, while ivy represented femininity) used it liberally at Saturnalia, their late December feast in honor of Saturn, father of the gods. Holly boughs were trained around doorways, windows, banquet tables, walking staves, and even the heads of celebrants.

As Christianity replaced Saturnalia with Christmas, it also appropriated the Saturnalian holly. First, however, holly had to atone for its pagan connotations.

The early Church in Rome spread the story that the scrubby holly bush was originally a proud tree with white berries. When the Romans were looking for wood for Jesus's cross, they chose to chop down a holly tree precisely because of its tall, straight, and smooth trunk. And when it came time to crown the King of the Jews in a suitably mocking ceremony, they wove a wreath of holly leaves and berries, and made it painfully tight. During the dark hours when Christ suffered on the cross, the blood pricked from his forehead by the sharp holly leaves stained the white holly berries red.

As legend goes, after Christ rose from the dead, all nature joyously celebrated his resurrection—except the remorseful holly tree. Overcome with shame, the holly tree vowed to do penance for its role in Christ's mortification by becoming Christ's tree. This meant remaining ever afterward a lowly bush with red berries, instead of a tall tree with white berries. It also meant that a certain amount of holly must give up its life each year to adorn homes, churches, and public places on Christ's birthday.

To many medieval Christians who believed this legend, the penance of the pagan holly tree gave the reformed holly plant new, magical powers. The Christian believers would mash holly leaves and berries in water and flour, and use the resulting paste as a poultice for speeding the recovery of rashes, poxes, burns, wounds, fractured bones, and congested lungs. They would boil an entire bough in water, and then drink that water to cure worms, colic, asthma, or gout. They would snip off leaves and berries from the holly that decorated their churches at Christmas, and keep these relics in an honored place at home all year long, to protect the house and everyone in it. The latter custom still survives, notably among the French and people of Creole descent in Louisiana.

However, to many Welsh believers, the holly was—and is—a plant to be scornfully disregarded except as a Christmastime decoration. If anyone should forget this prohibition and bring holly into his or her home *before* Christmas Eve, or leave it there *after* Twelfth Night, then it will cause family quarrels, and bring a separate misfortune for each and every leaf.

At any rate, the holly plant, too, has a claim to be called a Christmas tree. And Christmas halls decked with boughs of holly are definitely a tonic to the human spirit!

Christmas at Sea

true stories

❋   ❋   ❋

ifteen hundred years ago, Viking seamen used to tie a fir tree to the central mast of their boat before setting out on a long voyage. The tree functioned as a multifaceted talisman: a reminder of land, a tribute to Odin, father of the Norse gods, and a natural symbol of life everlasting. To this day, remnants of that tradition survive among different seafarers travelling in the north Atlantic Ocean, albeit without much reference to Odin.

For example, the "tree-mast" tradition can still be found in Provincetown, Massachusetts, where tireless and fearless fishermen of Portuguese descent have regularly fished the Great Banks off Newfoundland during the winter months, keeping New England and New York continuously supplied with fresh whiting and flounder. One of these Provincetown fishermen, Louis Rivers, is known as Christmas Tree Louis for keeping a pine tree lashed to the top of his mast. Each year, he replaces the old, dried-out pine tree with a fresh-smelling new one for the Blessing of the Fleet festival in May.

Another manner in which the "tree-mast" tradition has survived is in the common custom of erecting an evergreen tree aboard ship if the ship is at sea on Christmas, so that the tree can serve as the ship's major focal point during a special Christmas Day celebration. This custom had special meaning for those seamen of various nations who were engaged in the many nineteenth-century attempts to reach the North Pole. Such a journey typically lasted for at least two years, and the presence of a beloved natural landmark on board ship at Christmas helped to boost the sea-weary crew's morale.

One of the most noteworthy records of such a tree-oriented

This 1874 woodcut captures Christmas Eve, complete with tree, aboard the Vega, *an American research ship that regularly traveled the North Atlantic Ocean.*
(New York Public Library Picture Collection)

Christmas celebration comes from the 1870 Arctic expedition of the German ships *Germania* and *Hansa*. The two ships left Germany together, but became separated early in their voyage, before the onset of the annual winter freeze that compels all ships crossing the Arctic Ocean to seek temporary, land-based resting spots. As the 1870 winter freeze set in, the *Germania* anchored next to Sabine Island, just a few miles off the coast of Greenland. By that time, it had completely lost contact with the *Hansa*.

December in the Arctic circle may sound horrifically gloomy; but in fact, for Arctic expeditioners it could be a time of exceeding joy. With the ship itself firmly at rest, they could devote more time to relaxation and personal amusement. Moreover, they could see clear evidence that the long winter night of the Arctic circle was at last abating. Each day after December 21 (the winter solstice), the amount of daylight in the Arctic circle visibly expands day by day: from just a twilit half-hour at mid-day on December 21 itself, to an hour of full daylight by the end of January.

In 1870, around Sabine Island, December 21 marked the end of a terrible, weeklong storm. As soon as the sky cleared that morning, Doctor Pansch, botanist aboard the *Germania*, organized three teams of crew members to scour the dark and icy wastelands surrounding the ship for evergreens. Hours later, the three teams returned with basketloads of a bushy native evergreen known scientifically as *Andromeda tetragona*.

Dr. Pansch wound strands of this *Andromeda* evergreen around numerous small pieces of wood, then screwed the wooden pieces into a long pole, so that the pieces draped from the pole like branches. The result was a realistic-looking Christmas tree, which the crew trimmed with wax candles, gilded walnuts, and metal trinkets brought from home.

On Christmas Day, the Andromeda Tree was set up in the center of the dining hall, where crew members feasted on Sicilian wine and roast seal. At midnight, the tree was ceremoniously carried outside and used to start a bonfire. There ensued a "polar ball" on torchlit ice, with the men dancing two-by-two to an accordion played by the boatswain.

Meanwhile, the *Hansa* crew was not faring quite as well. The *Hansa* itself was crushed by shifting ice during the early days of the winter freeze, and so the crew spent Christmas camped out on a huge ice block, in huts constructed from the wreck debris. And yet Christmas Day itself was relatively festive—and a man-made Christmas tree stood at the center of the festivities!

The *Hansa* logbook for December 25, 1870, states:

> The tree was erected in the afternoon, while the greater part
> of the crew took a walk; and the lonely [dining] hut shone
> with wonderful brightness amid the snow. Christmas upon a
> Greenland iceberg! The tree was artistically put together of
> firwood and mat-weed, and Dr. Laube had saved a twist of
> wax-taper for the illumination.

That night, Dr. Laube, the illuminator himself, wrote in his diary:

We observed the day very quietly. If this Christmas be the last we are to see, it was at least a cheerful one; but should a happy return home be decreed for us, the next will, we trust, be far brighter. May God so grant.

God did so grant. All members of the *Hansa* crew were finally rescued after spending 200 days on their precarious block of ice.

Yet another heartwarming saga of Christmas on the frigid Arctic Ocean involves three Soviet Union ships on a polar expedition in 1937. All three ships were frozen into the ice before they had a chance to anchor themselves in a secure winter resting place.

Strictly speaking, ships in such a situation may wind up being no worse off than they might have been had they found a land-based berth, assuming the ice that holds them remains stable throughout the winter. But the danger that the ice may shift and crush the ship—as happened to the *Hansa* in 1870—is ever present. This danger kept the crew members of the three ice-locked Soviet Union ships on constant edge as the holiday season neared.

Within the Soviet Union, Christmas was not an officially recognized holiday. In fact, it was an officially *repressed* holiday. However, the Communist government was unable to stamp out popular enthusiasm for the Christmas tree and other colorful trappings associated with Christmas, and so these trappings were officially reassociated with New Year's Day, instead of Christmas. The newborn New Year's tree was popularly dubbed the *yolka*.

On board the *Sadko*, flagship of the 1937 Arctic expedition, crew members complained over and over again about the absence of a *yolka* to celebrate the New Year. Hearing these sad laments, Nikolai Bekasov, the radio engineer, invited everyone to a special and surprising New Year's Eve party.

At the appointed hour, the partygoers assembled outside the closed doors of the ship's wardroom. When the doors were flung open, they were amazed to see a fully-bedecked *yolka*, ablaze with electric lights! Bekasov, dressed as Grandfather Frost (the revamped version of Father

Christmas), led the grateful crew in a dance around the *yolka*, singing the newly traditional *yolka* song:

> *What merriment, what merriment,*
> *We're here in happy throng.*
> *We greet you, yolka, gleefully,*
> *With season's gayest song.*

Only on close inspection did the partygoers realize that their *yolka* was human-made, rather than natural. Bekasov had torn apart worn-out deck brooms, had painstakingly constructed fir-like branches by gluing broom bristles to cut-off broomstick sections, and had attached these branches around a stout wooden beam. Then, after painting the home-made twigs green, he had limned each branch with white "cotton glass" to resemble snow. As an engineer, he had experienced no trouble rigging up tree lights from spare bulbs and wiring for the final, *yolka*-tree touch.

The *Sadko* crew members were so impressed with Bekasov's *yolka*— and with the safe escape of all three ships from the ice the following spring—that they preserved the *yolka* intact for the rest of the expedition, which turned out to be highly successful in advancing scientific knowledge of the Arctic world. Today, Bekasov's *yolka* is still in perfect condition, and can be admired by visitors to the St. Petersburg Arctic Museum in Russia, where Christmas is once again an officially recognized holiday.

The Good Saint Florentin

a French legend

❋   ❋   ❋

Several hundred years ago, when the regions of Alsace and Lorraine belonged to the kingdom of France, there lived a saintly man named Florentin, in a hermitage far inside the great forest of Hassloch. His heart, mind, and energy were dedicated to the children who lived in the villages around him. All through the day, he helped them with their lessons, told them stories, and soothed their troubles.

Two children in particular were dear to Saint Florentin: Lisel and Yerri. Whenever they came by his humble one-room shack, he always had some small but delightful gifts for them. Sometimes, he would give them wooden animals—he was an excellent carver. Other times, he would give them nuts or berries in small baskets made from grass—he was an accomplished weaver. On very special times, he would give them cakes of honey and flour—he was a clever cook.

In sum, Saint Florentin was a kind and resourceful man. And the chief beneficiaries of his kindness and resourcefulness were Lisel and Yerri.

As Christmas drew near one year, Florentin was troubled. Lisel and Yerri were getting older, and he knew that their opening lives might take them away from him very soon. He wanted to make this Christmas, when they were still close companions, the most memorable Christmas of all. But he didn't know how. He was so poor, and he could only do so much with the materials surrounding his isolated shack.

Then, on a bitter cold morning while Florentin was walking in the forest, he saw a tiny fir tree with icicles hanging from every branch. The icicles sparkled like diamonds. Suddenly, he knew what to do for Lisel and Yerri!

Saint Florentin brought the tiny tree home and nailed it to a stand. Then he tied wood carvings, nuts, and apples to the branches of the tree. Finally, he baked little cakes for the tree out of honey and flour. Each cake was in the shape of a cross within a circle. And so began the custom of hanging such  cakes on a Christmas tree, a custom which is still followed in these parts.

But as Florentin had been busy trimming the little tree, it had lost the one feature that had first attracted him to it—its shiny icicles. They had melted away entirely. What could he do to make the tree sparkle again?

As he thought about it, he put his finger to his lips and tasted the honey that he used in the cakes. That was it! He went out to the beehive he kept in back of his shack and took a honeycomb from it. In this honeycomb, he found wax to make little candles, which he placed on the tree.

Christmas Eve was the next night. All about him, he could hear the bells ringing in the churches and the monasteries, and he knew that Lisel and Yerri would be visiting soon. Sure enough, before the bells stopped pealing, he heard their knocks on his door. He threw the door open, and the children gasped. The tree sparkled with light even more beautifully than it had in the forest. What's more, it was loaded with the kind of simple, loving presents that they most valued in the world!

Lisel and Yerri rushed inside to embrace Saint Florentin and to gather their gifts from the tree. In their haste, they left the door ajar. One by one, animals came to the door and gazed inside: fox and squirrel, wolf and deer, hawk and mouse. And because animals can talk on Christmas night—a miracle that began among the animals watching Christ's birth—Lisel and Yerri heard them murmuring about the wondrous new creation, the Christmas tree.

It was a Christmas that Lisel and Yerri never forgot. Nor did the people of these parts, who still light Christmas trees for the children.

The Nightingale and the Tree

a true story

❄   ❄   ❄

Jenny Lind (1820-1887), nicknamed the "Swedish nightingale" for her native Sweden, is remembered today as the most beloved soprano of her time. The amazing range of her voice and her repertoire—she was a gifted singer of popular melodies, as well as an accomplished opera star—won her a uniquely broad audience and long-lasting reputation. Few realize that she was also one of the early popularizers of the modern-era Christmas tree.

In addition to being a very warm, home-loving person, Lind was very proud of her Scandinavian heritage. These two personality traits combined to give her a special affection for the Christmas tree, the centerpiece of domestic celebration during the Swedish Christmas season. Whenever her professional travels took her away from home during Christmas, she had a proper Swedish Christmas tree set up in her hotel suite, decorated with silver paper, tiny apples, sugar cookies, and tassel candy (tube-shaped candy wrapped in colored paper with fringed ends).

In 1850, P. T. Barnum arranged for Lind to tour the United States: a tour that not only made her one of the first intercontinental singing sensations in history, but also promoted the songs of Stephen Foster, a composer she much admired. In a poster advertising this tour, she is depicted standing in front of a Christmas tree.

Linking Jenny Lind with a Christmas tree was no doubt a typically shrewd ploy by Barnum to bring out the common touch in Lind, and at the same time suggest a certain amount of exoticism, since most Americans at that time still considered a Christmas tree to be a foreign commodity. Perhaps Barnum also wanted the image of a tree to trigger subliminal recall of Lind's well-known "nightingale" nickname. In any event, both poster and singer captured the public imagination.

Christmas week in 1850, Lind was scheduled to perform in Charleston, South Carolina. Whether prompted by Barnum or their own Southern graciousness, a ladies' committee representing the city surprised Lind on Christmas Eve by erecting a Christmas tree outside one of the windows of her hotel suite. And it was no ordinary tree, but a tree brilliantly lit by dozens of Christmas lights suspended from its limbs.

Even Lind, a devotee of the Christmas tree, had never seen such lights before! A fairly new product in 1850, a Christmas light was a glass tumbler illuminated from within by a wick attached to a piece of cork floating on oil. Individual lights might be clear or colored, smooth or faceted, but the basic effect was the same: beautifully gleaming candlelight that was not only protected from drafts, but also much less likely to start a fire.

The most touching story involving Lind's love affair with the Christmas tree, however, took place five years earlier, when she was performing in Berlin. The story involves another famous Scandinavian, Hans Christian Andersen, who was also staying in Berlin for professional reasons and missing Christmas at home. Andersen recorded in his autobiography how bereft, how treeless, he felt on that Christmas Eve:

> I suddenly felt the power of loneliness, in its most oppressive form—Christmas Eve, the exact evening on which I always feel most festive, feel so glad to stand beside a Christmas-tree, enjoy so much the happiness of the children, and love to see the elders become children again . . . I sat quite alone in my window and looked up at the star-bespangled heavens. That was the Christmas-tree that had been lighted up for me.

These words are particularly ironic in light of the fact that Andersen had just written his classic Christmas tree tale, "The Fir Tree."

When word reached Lind that Andersen had passed Christmas Eve 1845 all by himself, instead of with friends or patrons as she had assumed, she planned a surprise party for her "brother" (in those days,

Scandinavians in general addressed each other as "brother" or "sister").
Andersen describes the event later in his autobiography:

> On the last evening of the year a little tree, with lights and
> pretty presents, was prepared for me alone—and that by Jenny
> Lind. . . . With sisterly feeling, she rejoiced over my success in
> Berlin, and I felt almost vain of the sympathy of so pure, so
> womanly a being. Her praises were sounded everywhere, the
> praises, not of the artist only, but of the woman.

The Spider Web Tree

a Ukrainian folktale

❄ ❄ ❄

All of her life, Katya had worked as a servant for the well-to-do Stepanski family. The Stepanskis were not exactly strict taskmasters, but they were not exactly kind taskmasters either. Katya's pay was stingy, and her hours were long. She was even required to work late on Christmas Eve, tending to the Stepanski family party, instead of being with her own fatherless son and daughter as she should be.

Above all else, a proper Ukrainian household had to be spotlessly clean from top to bottom on Christmas Day, ready to receive the newborn spirit of the Christ Child. And so Katya washed the walls, scrubbed the floors, waxed the furniture, and scraped out the chimney flues with bunches of stiff butcher's paper. Nevertheless, she went out of her way never to harm any spider she saw, for she held fast to the age-old belief that a spider in the house at Christmastime means good luck for the coming year.

In addition to the Christmas cleaning, there was the Christmas "charming" to do. Katya braided brightly colored strings around each leg of the dining table, so that the Stepanski fruit trees might not break by ice, wind, disease, or vandalism. She polished a small axe until it clearly reflected her face, and then laid it under the table, so that the Stepanski farm tools might be saved from rust and ruin. She spread clean hay on the floors of the children's rooms, so that the children would remain properly humbled by the lowliness of Christ's birth. She bound a sheaf of grain and decorated it with ribbons and tiny basil wreaths, so that it might stand beneath the Stepanski icon to ensure a good harvest. And in all these labors, she took pains not to disturb a single spider.

As if these labors weren't enough, Katya also had a full day's worth of cooking chores. A specially braided loaf of bread had to be baked for the traditional blessing ritual. As soon as the sun set, Father Stepanski would insert a candle into the loaf and, with the loaf held high in his hands, lead the entire family three times clockwise around the house, as they all said prayers for the well-being of the Stepanski family. Besides the braided bread, Katya had to prepare twelve traditional courses to serve to the family for Christmas Eve supper. And throughout her toils in the kitchen, she never mistreated any spider that crossed her path.

Finally, Katya had to dress the Christmas tree. Unlike the other tasks, however, this was a task that she truly loved. With great reverence and artistry, she tied small tapers of the best quality beeswax to the largest branches of the tree, counterbalancing every taper with a weighted ball so that it stood safely and securely upright. Then she decked the entire surface of the tree with delicate lace ribbons, expertly carved wooden figures of the saints, and finely tooled metal stars to reflect the candlelight.

When Katya finished decorating the Christmas tree to her satisfaction, she stood back and thrilled to the spectacle. She imagined the tree all alight and ringed with wondrous presents to delight the hearts of children. And then tears welled in her eyes as she thought of how poor a Christmas her own son and daughter would have. She resolved then and there that her children would at least have a Christmas tree to enjoy, however simple it might be.

By the time Katya left the Stepanskis that night, it was pitch black outside, and bitter cold. She should have headed straight home, but instead she detoured through the deep forest to find just the right tree to bring back for her children: small enough to fit inside their cramped, one-room cabin, and yet fragrant, full, and well shaped.

It took Katya quite a while to discover the perfect tree, and then to retrieve the axe from home and cut it down. By the time she set up the tree in the corner of her cabin, right next to her soundly sleeping children, there was only an hour left until daybreak. With nothing worthy at hand to adorn the tree, she said her prayers, lay down on her straw pallet, and instantly fell asleep.

Katya was awakened soon thereafter by the first shaft of daylight.

"My goodness, it's so bright!" she thought, as her dazzled eyes struggled to focus. And then she beheld the most wondrous sight she had ever seen in her whole hardworking life. The entire tree was covered with a beautiful network of spiderwebs, glistening in the light! By the time the sun rose fully in the sky, and her children began stirring in their beds, the webs had turned into pure silver.

To this day, mindful of the spiders' magical gift to Katya, Ukrainians consider a spider in the house to be a good luck omen at Christmastime. What's more, they adorn their Christmas trees with spiderweb ornaments, made from yarn, lace, wood, wire, and, in the case of some well-to-do Ukrainians, even silver!

The Christmas Tree Ship

a true story

✳   ✳   ✳

A century ago and then some, the Christmas season in Chicago, Illinois, was cold, windy, and snowy, just as it usually is now. But given the state of transportation back then, people in general suffered more because of the bad weather conditions. Going from place to place required far more exposure and vulnerability to the elements, whether one was engaged in commercial traffic or simply going about one's own business.

The outdoor harshness of nineteenth century Chicago at Christmastime made indoor coziness all the more valuable. And so the decorated Christmas tree, introduced throughout the Great Lakes region during the 1860s by a large wave of German immigrants, was an instant success. By the 1880s, the Christmas tree had gained widespread popularity among Chicagoans of every ethnic extraction.

August and Herman Schuenemann (SHOO-nee-mahn), two young and enterprising brothers from northern Michigan, took note of Chicago's increasingly heavy demand for evergreen trees at Christmastime and decided to capitalize on it. In the woods behind the Michigan towns of Manistique and Thompson grew vast numbers of young spruce trees. They had thrived on the land cleared by the previous generation to make lumber for houses in the newly settled Midwest. The brothers decided to transport some of these trees to Chicago, thus creating one of the very first long-distance, tree-selling ventures west of New York City.

In 1887, August and Herman Schuenemann began cutting the best-looking spruces around Manistique and Thompson six weeks before Christmas, when the branches were already enshrouded in snow. Two weeks later, they sailed to Chicago in a fishing schooner with the cut

trees lashed to the deck. They docked at a pier near the Clark Street Bridge and sold their entire shipload of trees—tree by tree—within a few days. Averaged out, they made 75¢ a tree. It wasn't a big profit, but a welcome one, considering the fact that the adverse winter weather conditions prohibited hauling most other cargoes.

Indeed, the cruel Lake Michigan winter soon took a heavy toll on the Schuenemanns, who continued to expand their Christmas tree service to Chicago from year to year thereafter. In early December 1898, August Schuenemann gave his younger brother Herman a goodby hug and set sail from Manistique with the first load of trees for that Christmas season. Only a few hours later, a fierce storm swept up and immediately sank the ship, leaving a swath of broken planks and evergreen needles to mark the spot where August drowned.

Herman Schuenemann was devastated by August's tragic death, but adamant about continuing the annual Christmas tree run. His motive wasn't profit: The overall income remained fairly modest. Instead, he now considered the business to be a memorial to his lost brother, as well as a means of spreading Christmas joy in the booming city he had come to love so much.

Then came the especially brutal winter of 1912. Despite strong head winds and choppy water, Herman Schuenemann loaded his schooner *Rouse Simmons*—now famous around Lake Michigan as "The Christmas Tree Ship"—on the prescheduled November day, and sailed out of Manistique harbor with a crew of seventeen men. Exactly what happened to the ship after leaving the harbor is still not fully known, but the ship never made it to Chicago that year.

Even before the *Rouse Simmons* was due to dock in Chicago, there were reports indicating trouble, though the weather remained fairly calm. On December 1, a land-based sentry near Kewaunee, Wisconsin, said that he had sighted a schooner resembling the *Rouse Simmons* two miles offshore, flying distress signals. On December 5, fishermen near Two Rivers Point, Wisconsin, found cut spruce trees tangled in their nets—a difficult phenomenon to explain, unless, of course, the trees had somehow drifted away from a ship at sea. And on December 13, a man walking the beach at Sheboygan, Wisconsin, allegedly picked up a bottle containing a page torn from a ship's log:

> Friday—Everybody goodbye. I guess we are all through. Sea washed over our deckload Thursday. During the night, the small boat washed over. Leaking bad. Ingvald [Nylons, a seaman] and Steve [Nelson, first mate] fell overboard Thursday. God help us.
>
> HERMAN SCHUENEMANN

No one but the person who claimed to have found the note ever saw it; but whether or not it actually existed, its message inspired a public outcry. Well aware of Herman Schuenemann's popularity as the captain of the Christmas Tree Ship, newspapers in Chicago and other cities bordering Lake Michigan published frantic and incessant rescue appeals. Search missions were conducted throughout December 1912 and January 1913. Cargo ships were diverted from their regular runs, private yachts volunteered, and revenue cutters were provided by the federal government.

Eventually, Herman Schuenemann's widow convinced herself that her husband and all the crew were dead, and she called off the hunt. But, like her husband before her, she was determined *not* to put an end to the Christmas Tree Ship itself.

On a sparkling, sunlit day in mid-December 1913, a new Christmas Tree Ship appeared at the customary Clark Street Bridge dock, loaded with spruces from upstate Michigan. Captaining the ship was Mrs. Schuenemann herself, accompanied by her daughters—Elsie, Pearl, and Hazel—and several other women prepared to weave Christmas wreaths and garlands for sale. With Mrs. Schuenemann supervising every detail, the Christmas Tree Ship continued to visit Chicago for another 22 years, until Mrs. Schuenemann grew too old to run it herself.

For a long time after the loss of the *Rouse Simmons*, no trustworthy clue to its fate emerged. On April 23, 1924, however, Lake Michigan at last yielded one. The wallet of Herman Schuenemann was discovered on a beach near Two Rivers Point, Wisconsin, where the fishermen of 1912 had dredged up cut spruce trees in their nets. Inside the wallet were newspaper accounts of pre-1912 voyages of the Christmas Tree Ship.

Three years later, in 1927, a bottle containing a note was picked up on a deserted shoreline not far away from Two Rivers Point. The note was signed by Charles Nelson, the seaman brother of the *Rouse Simmons'* first mate Steve Nelson, and read:

> These lines were written at 10:30 P.M. [no date]. Schooner R.S. ready to go down about 20 miles southeast Two Rivers Point between fifteen or twenty miles off shore. All hands lashed to one line. Goodbye.

And so the mystery of the lost Christmas Tree Ship, still not fully solved, was at least laid to rest. But the memory of the Christmas Tree Ship, a beloved Chicago institution for 47 years, remains ever green.

The Wild Woman of Albany

an American legend

❄ ❄ ❄

Close to Albany, New York, stands a large grove of evergreens that receives extraordinary attention at Christmas time. People journey there from up and down the Hudson Valley to festoon the branches of the trees with popcorn balls, strings of cranberries and marshmallows, wire-meshed blocks of suet and seeds, pine cones coated with peanut butter, orange peel cornucopias filled with dried fruit, and even doughnuts trimmed with ribbons! They are all honoring Agnes, the wild woman of Albany. Or, rather, they are honoring the wild creatures that Agnes loved.

A virtual hermit for the better part of her life, Agnes died at an indeterminately old age just as the nineteenth century was turning into the twentieth century. Her mental state had been unstable for so long, and she had so far outlived most of the generation into which she'd been born, that no one knew for sure how Agnes had come to live in the wild way she had.

Legend states that Agnes grew up as the shy, gawky, and sole child of an Albany merchant who had built up a lucrative fur-dealing business after the War of 1812. Unlike her father, the young Agnes valued a live animal far more than a dead one. Being motherless and alone during the days, she spent hours communing with the cats, dogs, and caged birds in the family mansion, and with the carriage horses in the family stable.

If Agnes shunned traveling in the smart social circles of Albany that were by rights her domain, she loved hiking through the many different kinds of wildlife habitats to be found in that part of the United States: riverbanks, lake shores, marshes, meadows, farmlands, forests, and mountainscapes. She always took along food for the animals and, whenever possible, brought wounded creatures back to the mansion so that she could nurse them to health. The locals laughed at her. They were not surprised that she remained unmarried—even unwooed—long after all the other women her age had husbands and children of their own.

Then something happened that astonished everyone. The most eligible bachelor in town, a handsome banker who had charmed all the women in Albany since moving there two years previously, began courting Agnes! Suddenly, drab, reclusive Agnes was transformed. At every Christmas party that winter, she dressed so prettily, and smiled so winningly, and danced so delightedly, that she looked beautiful. Only six months after they met, Agnes and the handsome bachelor married, and the people of Albany were unanimous in judging her to be the luckiest bride they had ever known.

But Agnes's luck turned quickly and cruelly. A year later to the day, her husband disappeared with every cent of the bank deposits, including her own family's millions, which she had transferred to the bank shortly after her wedding. Ruined and disgraced, her father succumbed to a massive heart attack that very week.

Many thought it would have been better for Agnes if she had suffered the same fate as her father. Realizing now that her cherished husband had only married her to get his hands on her fortune, she watched griefstricken as all her personal and family possessions, including the mansion itself, disappeared into the hands of creditors.

For many years afterwards, Agnes remained in Albany, living in a one-room hovel in the poorest sector of town, next to the docks on the Hudson where her father's fur-laden boats had once berthed. Out of pride, she refused to accept money, lodging, employment or even food from the few friends who offered it. Instead, shunning anyone and anything that reminded her of her former station, she cared for sick and injured domestic animals as best she could, and thereby earned a meager subsistence.

Finally even this threadbare lifestyle was more than she could manage, and she moved to a small, ramshackle cabin tucked into a grove of evergreens in the country outside Albany. The cabin had formerly belonged to a berry picker, and she had often noticed it during her girlhood nature walks.

Now Agnes herself began picking berries and selling them. She also braided evergreen boughs for Christmas decorations. As she entered old age, most of her free time was spent the same way that she had spent her youth: observing, feeding, and caring for wildlife, until she herself became somewhat like a wild animal.

Nevertheless, Agnes did have a few regular visitors from the civilized world. Animal lovers who had once benefited from her services came by to seek her advice and to look after her needs, and, as one year followed another, so did good-hearted younger souls who had heard of her, and who shared her love of animals. During the cold winter months, her visitors couldn't help but notice all the ingenious ways she'd devised for hanging food in the surrounding evergreens, so that the birds, squirrels, and other small creatures who were still out and about would not have to risk dying.

Other people drew close to Agnes in her last years—not welcome visitors, but unwelcome neighbors. Throughout the last quarter of the nineteenth century, much of the wilderness area around Albany was converted into private estates and public resorts. One resort developer eventually bought a huge tract of land that included Agnes's grove of evergreens. Not a completely heartless man, the developer agreed to postpone clearing the grove until after Agnes had died. He didn't have long to wait. A few months later, on a bitter cold night in mid-November, Agnes passed away.

People who had known Agnes continued to visit the grove during the weeks after her death to leave food for the animals on the trees. In

fact, newspaper accounts in early December about Agnes's legendary life and her love of animals had made her such a celebrity that many strangers showed up at the grove with their own personalized offerings of food.

The escalating number of food-bearing pilgrims to Agnes's grove created quite a dilemma for the developer. How was he to cut down the best-looking trees before Christmas, in time to adorn the great hall of his lodge for the holiday season, without provoking a public outcry from the recently bereaved friends of "the wild woman of Albany?"

The developer decided to send treecutters to the grove in the middle of the night just a few days before Christmas. No potential protestor, he reasoned, would be snooping around at such a late hour, and everyone would be so distracted that week by the nearness of Christmas that the damage to the grove would go relatively unremarked.

As the small team of treecutters approached the grove on the appointed night, clouds covered a full moon. Then the clouds broke, illuminating the grove and stopping the treecutters dead in their tracks.

Instead of evergreen trees, the treecutters saw live pyramids of birds, covering the trees so completely that not a single green branch was visible. Instead of a needle-strewn forest floor around the trees, the treecutters beheld a living carpet of fur: a tightly-packed army of squirrels, skunks, raccoons, and every other kind of small woodland creature not actually hibernating for the winter. And all the wild eyes on the trees and all the wild eyes on the forest floor gleamed in the moonlight, and stared directly at them!

Completely terrified, the treecutters ran from the scene. For days afterward they shared their story at Christmas gatherings with anyone who would listen, sometimes embellishing it with a full-fledged attack by the animals, or with the ghostly appearance atop the tallest tree of a resplendent angel, with robes of gossamer and the face of a radiant, youthful Agnes.

Newspaper reporters listened well to the treecutters' tales, and, under heavy pressure, so did the developer. To this day, the evergreen grove tended by Agnes, the wild woman of Albany, has never been harmed, nor have the animals who have lived near the grove ever gone without their Christmastime feasts.

The Tree Ornament Capital of the World

a true story

❄   ❄   ❄

Early in the 1840s, the Thuringian village of Lauscha, sixty miles north of Nuremberg in present-day Germany, gave birth to the Christmas tree ball. Specifically, the ball was the brainchild of a Christmas-loving glassblower seeking to develop his own self-sufficient cottage industry.

The independent glassblower hadn't counted on how wildly—and instantly—popular his simple, lacquered creation would be. Both adult and child Christmas tree decorators were enchanted by the way that the shiny opaque ball caught the flickering candlelight and sent it glimmering into the dark needled depths of the tree. Word of the marvelous new ornament spread quickly across Europe and across the Atlantic Ocean to America.

Over the next few years, most of the other artisans in Lauscha also began producing blown-glass Christmas tree balls. Within two decades, this storybook mountain village nestled deep in a forest of towering evergreens had gained international fame as the "Tree Ornament Capital of the World."

Lauscha glassblowers held a virtual monopoly on the Christmas tree ball market until World War I. After that, similar businesses sprang up in Austria, Poland, Czechoslovakia, and Japan, all places where glassblowing was a well-established and thriving art. But throughout the 1920s and 1930s, no other village, town, or city came close to challenging Lauscha's proud title.

During a visit to Germany in 1937, Max Eckardt, a New York City-based importer of Lauscha-made ornaments since 1907, became convinced that Hitler would lead Germany to war, and ultimately catastrophe. Knowing that a sizeable number of Lauscha glassblowers had already repatriated to the United States and had found jobs at Corning Glass, Eckardt travelled to Corning, New York, to see if he could talk these glassblowers and their employer into transferring the Tree Ornament Capital of the World from Lauscha, Germany, to Wellsboro, Pennsylvania, home of an existing Corning facility that was suitable for glass ball production.

Eckardt's scheme was not a spur-of-the-moment inspiration, but rather a lifetime in the making. He was born in the tiny village of Oberlind, Thuringia, less than twenty miles from Lauscha, and grew up admiring the Lauscha ornaments and ornament-making businesses. Shortly before World War I, he emigrated to the United States, and went to work in New York City for a toy vendor who also sold tree ornaments made in Lauscha. By 1926, Eckardt was the owner of his own business, specializing in the manufacture and importation of wooden toys and glass Christmas tree ornaments.

At the time that Eckardt proposed his ornament-producing idea to Corning, the company held exclusive patents to a new glassblowing technology that made electric light bulbs faster and better than they had ever been made previously. Eckardt was speculating that the same technology could be applied to making Christmas tree balls faster and better than the Lauscha balls themselves were made. He convinced Woolworth's, the department store chain, to promise Corning a huge order for the balls, if the technology could be successfully adapted.

That promise cinched the deal. In December 1938, 200,000 Corning-made Christmas tree balls were shipped to Woolworth's. Eckardt had been right: The Corning technology could make more tree balls in one minute than any German manufacturer could make in an entire day.

Corning's ornament-producing business was an overnight success, expanding geometrically over the next few years, but it couldn't survive the increasing shortage of needed materials caused by World War II. Midway through the war, Eckardt's own company took over the production of glass Christmas tree ornaments on a much smaller scale, marketing them under the brand name Shiny Brite. When Eckardt could no longer get silver and lacquer to decorate the glass balls, he substituted painted stripes. When he could no longer get metal for the hangers, he substituted cardboard. Almost singlehandedly, his firm made sure that America didn't go without Christmas tree balls during the long last years of World War II.

After the war, Shiny Brite became the biggest Christmas tree ball producer anywhere on the globe, and it remained the biggest producer into the 1960s. To avoid the danger of losing his entire manufacturing capability to an explosion (a major risk for industries working with silver nitrate and lacquer), Eckardt built factories in four different New Jersey locations. Thus, from 1945 to 1968, the state of New Jersey was The Tree Ornament Capital of the World.

In 1949, Eckardt journeyed on a goodwill mission to West Germany, to see if he could help start a new ornament-making industry there. Few glassblowing businesses had survived the war in Lauscha.

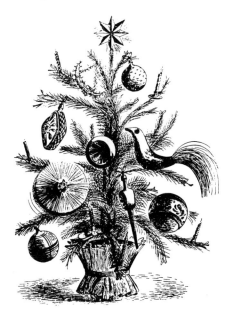

Besides, Lauscha was now ten miles inside East Germany. Not only was it cut off from Western markets, but Christmas itself—the very holiday on which it had based its livelihood for almost a century—was outlawed by the communist East German government.

With Lauscha officially out of the business, there was little that Eckardt could do but help establish small export businesses dealing in the special kinds of hand-blown, hand-decorated ornaments that could never be produced by machines. Meanwhile, a black market developed for the relatively few ornaments Lauscha still managed to produce.

Philip V. Snyder, a well-known authority on Christmas tree ornaments, offers a touching picture of this black market in his fascinating 1976 work, *The Christmas Tree Book* (NY: Viking Press):

> On foggy nights Lauscha men stealthily carried baskets, old
> suitcases, and bundles of their fragile glass ornaments rolled in
> tablecloths to silent border meetings, where the ornaments
> were slipped under the barbed-wire fence. In return, they got
> razor blades, coffee, cigarettes, and other commodities hard to
> obtain in the eastern zone.

This pathetically furtive and small scale trading represented quite a dramatic comedown for Lauscha from having been The Tree Ornament Capital of the World only two decades before.

Toward the end of the 1960s, Corning resumed production of its own Christmas tree ornaments. Because of the huge size of the company, and the resulting economy with which it was able to produce and market Christmas tree balls, its production soon surpassed that of Shiny Brite.

Today, Corning is responsible for most of the glass Christmas tree balls sold on the national and international market. And because Corning is an interstate company, the title of The Tree Ornament Capital of the World must now be applied to the United States as a whole.

The Fir Tree

a tale by Hans Christian Andersen

❄   ❄   ❄

Deep in the forest, where the warm sun and fresh air made a nice resting-place, grew a pretty little fir tree. And yet it was not happy. It yearned to be tall like the pines and firs that grew around it. The sun shone, and the soft air fluttered its branches, and the peasant children passing by prattled sweetly, but the fir tree didn't care. Sometimes the children would bring a large basket of raspberries, or strawberries wreathed on a straw, seat themselves near the fir tree, and exclaim, "How pretty the little fir tree is!" But this only made it feel more unhappy than before.

The fir tree grew a joint taller every year (for you can tell the age of a fir tree by counting the joints in its stem), and all the while it complained, "Oh, how I wish I were as tall as the other trees. Then I would spread out my branches, and my top would look over the whole, wide world. Birds would built their nests in my boughs; and when the wind blew, I should bow with stately dignity!" So discontented was the tree that it took no pleasure in the sunshine, the flying birds, or the rosy clouds that sailed above it from dawn to dusk.

In the winter, when the snow lay glittering all around it, a hare would sometimes jump right over the little tree, and how mortified it would feel! Two winters passed, and when the third came, the tree had grown so tall that the hare had to run around it. But still, it was unsatisfied. "Oh, if I could only keep on growing taller and older!" it sighed. "Nothing else matters!"

In the autumn, the woodcutters came and cut down several of the tallest trees. The fir tree, now grown to a respectable size, shuddered as they fell. After their branches were lopped off, the trunks looked so thin and bare that they couldn't be recognized. Then, they were loaded on wagons and hauled away by horses. "Where are they going?" the fir tree wondered. "What will become of them?"

In the spring, the storks and the swallows came, and the fir tree asked them, "Do you know where those trees were taken? Have you met them anywhere?" The swallows knew nothing, but then a stork nodded and said, "Yes, I think so. I met several ships when I flew from Egypt, and they had fine masts that smelled like fir. These must have been the trees! I assure you, they were very majestic!"

"Oh, how I wish I were tall enough to go to sea!" cried the fir tree. "What is the sea, and what does it look like?"

"That would take too long to explain!" said the stork, and he flew away.

"Rejoice in your youth," counseled the sunbeams. "Rejoice in your fresh growth, and the life that is in you!" And the wind kissed the tree, and the dew watered it with tears; but the fir tree would not be comforted.

Christmas drew near, and many trees were cut down, some even smaller than the restless fir tree, who longed to leave the forest. These young trees, which were chosen for their beauty, kept their branches, but they were also laid on wagons and hauled away by horses. "Where are they going?" wondered the fir tree. "They are not all taller than I am, and their branches are not cut off. Oh, where are they going?"

"We know, we know," sang the sparrows. "We have peeked in the windows of houses, and we know what is done with them. They are dressed up in the most splendid manner. We have seen them standing in the middle of a warm room, adorned with beautiful things like honey cakes, gilded apples, playthings, and hundreds of wax tapers!"

"And then what happens?" asked the fir tree, trembling through every branch.

"That's all we saw," replied the sparrows, "but that was enough for us!"

"Oh, will anything so brilliant ever happen to me?" thought the fir tree. "I would much prefer that, rather than crossing the sea. I long for it almost with pain! When will Christmas be here? I am as tall as many of the trees that were carried off. Oh, that I were now laid on that wagon,

or standing in that warm room, with all the brightness and splendor around me! Surely something better comes after, or the trees would not be so beautifully dressed! Yes, what follows must be even grander! Oh, I can't wait!"

"Rejoice with us," said the sunbeams and the wind. "Enjoy your own bright life in the fresh air!" But the tree would not rejoice. Instead, it grew taller every day; and passersby, admiring its dark green foliage, would murmur, "What a beautiful tree!"

Shortly before Christmas, the fir tree was the first to fall. As the axe cut its stem, it toppled to the earth with a groan, forgetting all its expectations of happiness, and grieving for its lost home in the forest. It knew it would never see the other trees again, nor the little bushes and flowers that had grown by its side—perhaps not even the birds. Nor was the journey itself a pleasant one.

The fir tree began recovering while it was being unpacked in the courtyard of a house with several other trees, and heard a man pointing to it declare, "We want only one, and this is the prettiest." Then came two liveried servants, who carried the fir tree into a large and beautiful apartment. On the walls hung paintings, and near the great stove stood handsome china vases, with lions on the lids. There were rocking chairs, silken sofas, and tables covered with pictures, books, and playthings worth a fortune—or at least the children said so.

Then the fir tree was placed in a tub full of sand; but pretty green baize hung around the tub so that no one could see what it was, and it stood on a luxurious carpet. How the fir tree trembled with anticipation! What was going to happen to it now?

Some young ladies and servants entered the room and began adorning the tree's branches. On some branches they hung little bags cut out of colored paper and filled with sweetmeats. On others, they hung gilded apples and walnuts, as if they had grown there. And all around they fastened hundreds of red, blue, and white tapers. Dolls, exactly like babies, were placed underneath the lowest branches—the fir tree had never seen such things—and at the very top, they hung a glistening gold star. Everything was so marvelous!

"How brightly the tree will shine this evening!" exclaimed the young ladies. "Oh, that the evening would come," thought the tree, "and the tapers would be lighted! Then I shall know what else is going to happen. Will forest trees come to see me? Will the sparrows peek in the windows? Shall I grow faster here, and keep on all my ornaments?" But guessing was useless, and made its bark ache, which is as painful for a tree as a headache is for us.

At last the tapers were lit, and then what a glittering blaze of light the tree presented! It shook so with joy that one of the candles fell and set fire to a branch. "Help! Help!" cried the young ladies, and the fire was quickly put out. After this, the bedazzled and bewildered tree was afraid to move, lest it lose some of its splendor.

Suddenly, the drawing room doors were thrown open, and a troop of children rushed in as if they intended to tackle the tree. Their elders soon followed, and for a while everyone silently admired the tree. Then they shouted for joy till the room rang, and danced merrily around the tree, and plucked their presents from its branches.

"What are they doing?" thought the tree. "What will happen now?" The candles finally burned down and were put out. Then the children were given permission to plunder the tree for its candy, cakes, and fruits. How they rushed upon it, until the branches cracked; and if it had not been fastened securely to the ceiling with the shiny gold star, it would certainly have tumbled down. Afterwards, the children played around it with their new toys, and no one noticed it, except the maid who came and peeked among the branches for a fig or apple that had been forgotten.

"A story! A story!" cried the children, drawing a little fat man towards the tree. He seated himself under it and said, "Now we shall be in the green shade, and the tree will have the pleasure of hearing also. But I shall tell only one story. What shall it be? Ivedy-Avedy or Humpty-Dumpty?"

"Ivedy-Avedy!" cried some. "Humpty-Dumpty!" cried others. But the fir tree remained quite still, and thought to itself, "Am I to have anything to do with all this?" Discouraged, it realized that it had already

done as much as they wanted it to do. Then the fat man told them the story of Humpty-Dumpty, how he fell down the stairs, and was raised up again, and married a princess. And the children clapped their hands and yelled, "Please tell another!" but Humpty-Dumpty was all.

The fir tree became quite thoughtful: Never had the birds in the forest told such tales as Humpty-Dumpty. "Ah, yes, that's the way things go," the tree decided. It believed the story, because the story had been related by such a nice man. "Perhaps I may fall down, too, and then marry a princess!" And it looked forward joyfully to the next evening, when it expected to be decked out again with lights, gold, cakes, fruit, and playthings. "Tomorrow I will not shake," it vowed. "I will enjoy all my spendor, and I shall hear Humpty-Dumpty again, and maybe even Ivedy-Avedy." And the tree remained quiet and hopeful all night long.

In the morning, the servants came in, and the tree thought, "Now all my splendor is going to begin again." But instead, they dragged it out of the room and up the stairs to a dark garret, where they threw it on the floor and left it. "What does this mean?" wondered the tree. What am I to do here?" Days and nights passed, and no one came up. It seemed as if the tree had been completely forgotten.

"It is winter now," the tree thought, "and the ground is hard. The people cannot plant me, so I am being sheltered here until the spring! How kind they are, after all! Still I wish this place were not so dark and lonely. How pleasant it was out in the forest when the snow lay on the ground, and when the hare would come by, even though I didn't like the hare then."

"Squeak, squeak," said a little mouse, creeping towards the tree. Then came another, and they both sniffed at the fir tree and crept between its branches. "It is awfully cold," said one mouse, "or we should be quite comfortable here, shouldn't we, old tree?"

"I am not old," answered the tree. "There are many trees older than I am!"

"Where do you come from, and what do you know?" asked the mice, who were full of curiosity. "Have you seen the most beautiful places in the world, and can you tell us about them? And have you been in the storeroom, where cheeses lie on the shelf, and hams hang from the ceiling? One can run about on tallow candle there, and go in thin and come out fat!"

"I know nothing of that place," said the fir tree, "but I know the wood, where the sun shines and the birds sing." And the tree told the mice all about its youth. They had never heard such an account in their lives; and after they had listened to it attentively, they said, "What a number of marvels you have seen! You must be very happy!"

"Happy?" exclaimed the fir tree, and then, after reflecting on the memories it had been telling them, it sighed, "Ah yes, after all, those were happy days!" But then it went on to relate all about Christmas Eve, and how it had been dressed up with cakes and lights, and the mice said, "How happy you must have been, you old fir tree!"

"I am *not* old," replied the tree. "I only came from the forest this winter."

"Well, anyway, what wonderful stories you can tell," chimed the mice. And the next night, four other mice came with them to hear what the tree had to say. The more it talked, the more it remembered, and then it thought, "Those were happy days, but they may come again. Humpty-Dumpty fell down stairs, and yet he married the princess. Perhaps I may marry a princess, too." And the fir tree thought of the pretty little birch tree that grew in the forest.

"Who is Humpty-Dumpty?" asked the little mice. And then the tree related the whole tale. It could recall every word, and the mice were so delighted that they were ready to jump to the top of the tree. The next night, a great many more mice appeared, and on Sunday, two rats came. But the rats said that the story wasn't very good, and the mice were sorry, for now they thought less of the story, too.

"Do you know only that one story?" asked the rats.

"Only that one," replied the tree. "I heard it on the happiest night of my life, but I did not know I was so happy at the time."

"We think it is a very miserable story," replied the rats. "Don't you know a story about bacon, or tallow in the storeroom?"

"No," replied the tree.

"Many thanks to you then," said the rats, and off they marched. The mice also kept away after this, and the tree sighed and said, "It was nice when the merry little mice sat all around me and listened while I talked. Now that is all passed. However, I shall consider myself happy when someone comes to take me out of this place." But would this ever happen?

Yes. One morning, the servants came up to clean the garret. The tree was dragged onto the outdoor staircase, where the sun shone. "Now life begins again!" it thought, rejoicing in the sun and the fresh air. Then it was carried down into the courtyard so quickly that it forgot to think of itself, and could only marvel at all that it saw.

The courtyard was next to a garden, where everything was in bloom. Fragrant roses hung over the little palings. The linden trees were heavy with blossoms. And the swallows flew here and there, crying, "Twit, twit, twit, my mate is coming." But they didn't mean the fir tree.

"Now I shall live!" cried the tree, joyfully spreading its branches. But alas! They were withered and yellow, and so it lay back motionless in its dirty corner among the weeds and nettles. The shiny gold star that still stuck in the top of the tree glittered in the sunlight. Two of the children who had danced around the tree at Christmas saw it there and pulled it off. "Look what is sticking to the ugly old fir tree!" said one of the children, who proceeded to tread on its branches till they cracked under his boots.

The tree looked at all the fresh bright flowers in the garden, then at itself, and wished it had remained in the dark garret. It thought of its pleasant childhood in the forest, of the merry Christmas evening, and of the little mice who had listened to it tell the story of Humpty-Dumpty. "Passed! All passed!" said the old tree. "Oh, if only I had enjoyed myself while I could have done so! Now it is too late!"

Then the gardener's lad came and chopped the tree into pieces, till a large heap of wood lay on the ground. The wood was tossed into a fire under a brewing copper, and it quickly blazed up, sighing so deeply that each sigh was like a pistol shot. The children stopped playing and seated themselves in front of the fire, one of them wearing the shiny gold star on his breast. They cried "Pop!" whenever the wood sighed, and the wood sighed often thinking of a summer day in the forest, of Christmas eve, and of telling Humpty-Dumpty to the mice. At last the tree was gone, and so is this story—for all stories must come to an end.

Your Own
Christmas Tree Story

inally, here is a gift story idea, a stimulus to develop your own storytelling talent. One of the most mysterious tree images associated with Christmas is the partridge-bearing pear tree in the carol, "The Twelve Days of Christmas." Indeed, the whole carol is mysterious. Why not make up a story—or a series of stories—to explain all the images in that carol?

Twelve lords a-leaping,
Eleven ladies dancing,
Ten pipers piping,
Nine drummers drumming,
Eight maids a-milking,
Seven swans a-swimming,
Six geese a-laying,
Five golden rings,
Four calling birds,
Three French hens,
Two turtle doves,
And a partridge in a pear tree.